KU-657-936

# Let Me Be a Woman

# Let Me Be a Woman

Notes on Womanhood
for Valerie

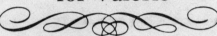

## Elisabeth Elliot

HODDER AND STOUGHTON

LONDON · SYDNEY · AUCKLAND · TORONTO

British Library Cataloguing in Publication Data
Elliot, Elisabeth
  Let me be a woman.
  1. Marriage
  I. Title
261. 8'34'2        HQ734

  ISBN 0 340 23349 4

First published in Great Britain 1979

*Printed in Great Britain for
Hodder and Stoughton Limited,
Mill Road, Dunton Green, Sevenoaks, Kent
by Cox & Wyman Ltd., London, Reading and Fakenham*

# Contents

# Foreword

A strong southwest wind blows across the harbor this morning, whipping the lilac bushes and honeysuckle in front of the cottage and sending the gulls steeply upward when they seem to mean to go down. The masts of the moored sailboats tip and swing, and the grey water flashes with whitecaps. There is no sound but the wind, the crying of the gulls, and, once in a while, the bell buoy, muffled and far away. It is a good morning to write to you, Val, better than the first two mornings I was here, for they were beautiful sunny mornings and I went across the road to the beach and walked with MacDuff. He raced joyfully along, his square muzzle sweeping the sand for new and exciting scents. Then he would stop, his gay Scotty tail and pointed ears erect, his nose lifted, every nerve aquiver as he waited for me to catch up with him, when off he would tear again. You know how he does.

Yesterday afternoon I found a quiet place on the sand, out of sight of any house, and sat with my back against a smooth granite rock. You were to have come with me to the Cape, but wonderful things happened to change that, and instead of being here you are with Walt. It was blissful sitting in the sun, looking out toward Nauset Beach across the harbor, thinking of your happiness. He will leave you today, I know, to take up his duties as a minister in Louisiana, and then you will leave for England to study, but you have had a few days with him and when you are engaged such days are unspeakably precious.

You and I will have four or five weeks together between now and your wedding day eleven months hence, and we will talk, but I know that there will not be time to speak of all we would like to, so I write you these notes.

You know, I'm sure, that the notes come not only out of my own experience of marriage. They come out of a lifetime, most of which has been spent single (I have been married, you know, for only a seventh of my life). They come out of being a woman, and seeking to be—single, married, widowed—a woman for God. The attitude with which this effort began is summed up in the prayer of Betty Scott Stam, copied into my Bible and signed when I was ten or eleven years old:

"Lord, I give up all my own plans and purposes, all my own desires and hopes, and accept Thy will for my life. I give myself, my life, my all utterly to Thee to be Thine forever. Fill me and seal me with Thy Holy Spirit. Use me as Thou wilt, send me where Thou wilt, work out Thy whole will in my life at any cost, now and forever."

# ONE

# The God Who Is in Charge

When Walt came to me at Christmastime to ask for your hand I said to him, "There is no one to whom I would so gladly give it." Then we talked of the long wait you would have if the wedding date was not to be until after your graduation.

"Do you think you can stick it out?" I asked him, and he answered, without hesitation, "Ma'am, I'm a Calvinist!"

He knew that I would understand what he meant by that. You and I are Calvinists too, in that we believe in a God who is in charge. We are not for one moment of our lives at the mercy of chance. Walt saw the timing of his proposal, his own graduation from seminary, your graduation from college, as among the "all things" that work together for good to those who love God. He saw the pattern of duty that lay before you both and took it to be the will of God, so that the power of his own emotion to weaken his resolve was not a threat. He knew, as the psalmist knew, "My flesh and my heart faileth, but God is the strength of my heart and my portion forever." I am grateful that God has given you a man like that.

# Not Who Am I? but Whose Am I?

These notes will all be, in one way or another, about the meaning of womanhood. Women during the past decade have contrived to place themselves very much in the center of attention. They are talked about, puzzled about, argued about, and legislated about and it is women who have done most of the talking, arguing, and perhaps the legislating, while it is men, I suppose, who have done more of the puzzling. A torrent of books about women has been pouring from the presses urging women to cast off traditional roles, to refuse the socialization that has for so many centuries, they say, controlled and confined them, and to move into what some of them call "human" (as distinct from biological or reproductive) pursuits, which, whether they are interesting or uninteresting are said to be male territory.

Is being a woman fundamentally different from being a man?

Is there anything inherent in the nature of human beings or of human society that requires certain roles or tasks to be associated with one sex or the other? Ought authority to be associated only or even mainly with men rather than women? Does it matter who runs things? Does bearing a child necessarily mean that the bearer should care for it? What is marriage? How does it work? Is a woman's lot really as bad as Germaine Greer says it is, "a lifetime of camouflage and idiotic ritual, full of forebodings and failure"?

Most of those who try to find answers for these questions start at the wrong place. They start with themselves. They ask "Who am I?" "How do I really feel?" and they assume that if enough people express their personal opinions on this subject we will all somehow arrive at the truth of the matter. Carlyle observed this tendency and wryly observed, "Vulpine knowingness sits ever at its hopeless task—from a world of knaves to deduce an honesty from their combined action."

There is, no doubt, a superficial sort of consolation and reassurance to be gained from sitting around telling how you feel about things. You generally find several others who feel the same way, or (what is even more reassuring and consoling) they feel worse than you do. But it is no way to come at the truth.

In order to learn what it means to be a woman we must start with the One who made her.

THREE

# Where to Hang Your Soul

Every Sunday morning in our church we repeat a creed. You know what it says. "I believe in one God, the Father, the Almighty, Maker of all things visible and invisible." There's a statement that has nothing whatever to do with my personal opinions or emotions. It's a statement of objective fact, accepted by faith, and when I stand up in the company of other Christians and repeat this statement I am not talking about myself at all. The only thing I am saying about myself is that I submit to these truths. This is where I stand, this is Reality.

Very often (nearly always, I'm afraid) when I come to church my feelings are uppermost in my mind. This is natural. We are human, we are "selves," and it takes no effort at all to feel. But worship is not feeling. Worship is not an experience. Worship is an act, and this takes discipline. We are to worship "in spirit and in truth." Never mind about the feelings. We are to worship in spite of them.

Finding my thoughts scattered in all directions and in need of corralling like so many skittish

14

calves, I kneel before the service begins and ask to be delivered from a vague preoccupation with myself and my own concerns and to be turned, during this short hour, to God. Often the words of the Jesus Prayer, which I learned from a book about a Russian pilgrim who spent his life seeking to know the full meaning of it, help in this "corralling":

"Lord Jesus Christ, Son of God, have mercy on me." Orthodox Christians pray this over and over, in the rhythm of breathing. This prayer has rescued me from wordlessness in many places quite different from church services.

When I stand to say the creed I am lifted up to eternal verities, far past the trivialities of how I feel, what I must do after church, what so-and-so said or did to me. I hang my soul on those strong pegs, those "I believe's." And I am strengthened.

Sometimes we sing St. Patrick's great hymn:

> I bind unto myself today
> The strong Name of the Trinity,
> By invocation of the same,
> The Three in One, and One in Three.
>
> I bind unto myself today
> The power of God to hold and lead,
> His eye to watch, his might to stay,
> His ear to hearken to my need.

If in fact I do believe these *great* things we say and sing together, then those *little* things (and what is not little by comparison?) will be taken care of. I take my position, I get my bearings. I need to do this

15

often—more often, it seems, in these days when so many have altogether lost their bearings.

# FOUR

# *A Daughter, Not a Son*

To understand the meaning of womanhood we have to start with God. If He is indeed "Creator of all things visible and invisible" He is certainly in charge of all things, visible and invisible, stupendous and miniscule, magnificent and trivial. God has to be in charge of details if He is going to be in charge of the overall design.

We sometimes hear the expression "the accident of sex," as though one's being a man or a woman were a triviality. It is very far from being a triviality. It is our nature. It is the modality under which we live all our lives; it is what you and I are called to be—called by God, this God who is in charge. It is our destiny, planned, ordained, fulfilled by an all-wise, all-powerful, all-loving Lord.

I had wanted a son. I had felt very sure that every man wants a son first, and it seemed logical to me to want the eldest to be a boy, an older brother, the firstborn, the heir. So we had prayed for a son and your father was quite certain that God would give him to us.

Your father was with me when you were born. I

could see his face when the doctor said, "It's a girl."
He smiled at me and said at once, "Her name is
Valerie." The nurse wrapped you in a little blanket
and laid you where I could look into your face, and
your eyes—darker blue then—were wide open, looking into mine. (How does a baby know to look at
another's *eyes*?) A person. Separate and independent now of me. My daughter.

Later they brought you to me and I held you and
then your father took you from my arms and held
you close and said, "Little dolly!" He was not given
to sentimentality or baby-talk, but there was no
other way to describe how you looked—pink cheeks
and lips, blue eyes, a silken fringe of light hair. Even
the doctor and nurse, a husband and wife who had
seven children of their own, said you were beautiful.

He was perfectly contented, I could see, to be the
father of a daughter instead of a son. So I was
content. It was God who had given you to us, God to
whom our prayers for a son had been made, and God
who knew reasons we did not then know that made
His choice far better.

If you believe in a God who controls the big
things, you have to believe in a God who controls the
little things. It is we, of course, to whom things look
"little" or "big." Amy Carmichael wrote:

> There is no great with Thee, there is no small,
> For Thou art all, and fillest all in all.

18

# Creation—
# Woman for Man

It has been an afternoon of wild wind, with the sun showing only for brief intervals through the scudding clouds. I wanted to be out in the wind, so MacDuff and I went to Nantucket Sound where we could run on a long, empty beach. The wind helped us as we ran, and we covered perhaps a mile before we turned around. Then the sand blew into our eyes and the wind held us back. I had to lean into it, and MacDuff flattened his ears and sneezed as sand plastered his muzzle. Halfway back I found a dune which would give us some shelter, and sat down. MacDuff was glad to sit beside me for a few minutes until it suddenly struck him that he ought to be digging. And dig he did, with furious energy, sending a blast of sand backwards from his powerful forepaws.

It is not hard to think of God's greatness when you look at the sea and an immensity of horizon and sky. It is not hard to think of the power of His imagination when you study the designs of shells. (I say it is not hard to *think* of it. It *is* hard—it is impossible—to comprehend it. As an Eighth Century Church father, John of Damascus, said, "God is infinite and incomprehensible and all that is comprehensible about Him is His infinity and incomprehensibility.") God is the Almighty, the Creator, a God of Order, Harmony, Design. We believe the creation story in the first two chapters of the Bible, and we delight in knowing that the Maker of all that list of marvels delighted when He looked at them. He made each thing according to the Word of His power, and when He looked at it, He saw that it was good.

He made man in His own image, and then for the first time God saw something that was not good. It was not good for the man to be alone. God determined to make a helper fit for him and it was after this decision, according to Genesis 2:19, that He made the animals and birds—as though from among them such a helper might be chosen. He even brought them to Adam, "to see what he would call them." Imagine the Almighty Creator waiting "to see" what His creature Adam might come up with for names! Adam came up with them, all right. The power of his imagination was impressive too. He thought of names for every one of the cattle, birds, and animals. And he and God must have looked them all over together.

What a scene that must have been—God and Adam looking the animals over. Did Adam, contemplating these other beings, have even a moment's identity crisis such as I would have had, asking, "Who am *I* compared with them?"

You and I love zoos. We stand and stare. We watched tigers mate once (a lady near us said, "Atta girl!" but a man said, "I'm getting out of here!") and once, staring at an elephant when you were three or four years old you finally said, "How come they have those things instead of feet?"

The animals stare back, their eyes meeting ours through the bars. Something infinitely greater than those bars separates us. There is a great gulf fixed, a fathomless mystery which I sometimes think the animals understand—they gaze with such serenity—but which reminds me of how bottomless is my own ignorance. Men capture, use, control, and kill animals. Sometimes they love them.

We love MacDuff. No other word will do. We love him. He is a good companion, perfectly silent when he is here in the house and I am working, perfectly ready to do whatever I decide we are going to do in the afternoons, and perfectly dedicated to his divinely appointed (yes, I think it was *appointed*) task of keeping me happy. Adam, I'm sure, loved the animals who were his companions in the garden. He might even have had a special friend in a dog or a horse or a unicorn. But what did he, what do we, understand?

I read just yesterday of a beautiful race horse who shattered her ankle and kept running the race, doing the thing she was trained to do, until at last she had to halt. They tried to fix it, but when she regained consciousness she threw off the cast in a frenzy of fear and pain. They had to destroy her. The magazine picture of that magnificent creature held by thin reins as she reared confounded me. Her obedience to trainers and jockey won money for her owners, suffering and death for her. No one could explain to her or apologize.

The animals are there, fellow-creatures with us of the same Creator-God, fellow-sufferers, mute and mysterious. "But for the man there was not found a helper fit for him."

God might have given Adam another man to be his friend, to walk and talk and argue with if that was his pleasure. But Adam needed more than the companionship of the animals or the friendship of a man. He needed a helper, specially designed and prepared to fill that role. It was a woman God gave him, a woman, "meet," fit, suitable, entirely appropriate for him, made of his very bones and flesh.

You can't make proper use of a thing unless you know what it was made for, whether it is a safety pin or a sailboat. To me it is a wonderful thing to be a woman under God—to know, first of all that we were *made* ("So God created man in his own image, in the image of God he created him; male and female he created them.") and then that we were made *for* something ("The rib which the Lord God had taken from the man he made into a woman and brought her to the man.").

This was the original idea. This is what woman was for. The New Testament refers back clearly and strongly to this purpose: "For man was not made from woman, but woman from man. Neither was man created for woman, but woman for man." Some texts are susceptible of differing interpretations, but for the life of me I can't see any ambiguities in this one.

# *Jellyfish and Pride*

When you were very small you used at times to say "some people" when you were really referring to yourself. One night when we were on board ship you were tucked into the upper berth and had just finished your evening prayers.

"God made everything in the world," you then said to me, "but some people don't know why He made jelly fish and tigers." You had been stung once by a jelly fish, and "tigers" were what you called the ocelots and jaguars that lived in the jungle where we were living. Indians were afraid of them and so, of course, were you. But you were not asking specifically *why* God made them. You did not understand it, but you were not admitting that you did not understand it. You were only observing philosophically that there were those who did not, and, tactfully, you were not suggesting that your mother might be among them. Your three-year-old mind could hardly have grasped the implications of the mystery you had touched on. For the answer would have to include, from a human standpoint, an explanation of human suffering. Yet the jelly fish and the tiger "know" what they were made for. They, with all sea monsters and all deeps, fire and hail, snow and frost, mountains and hills, beasts and all cattle, praise the Lord. By being a jelly fish the jelly fish glorifies its Creator, for by being a jelly fish it fulfills its Creator's command.

All creatures, with two exceptions that we know of, have willingly taken the places appointed to them. The Bible speaks of angels who rebelled and therefore were cast down out of heaven, and of the fall of man. Adam and Eve were not satisfied with the place assigned. They refused the single limitation set them in the Garden of Eden and thus brought sin and death to the whole world. It was, in fact, the woman, Eve, who saw the opportunity to be something other than she was meant to be—the Serpent convinced her that she could easily be "like God"—and she took the initiative. We have no way of knowing whether a consultation with her husband first might have led to an entirely different conclusion. Perhaps it might. Perhaps if she had put the question to him and he had had to ponder the matter he would have seen the deadly implications, and have refused the fruit. But Eve had already tried it. She had not been struck dead. She offered it to her husband. How could he refuse? Eve was undoubtedly a beautiful woman. She was the woman God had given him. She was only testing out what seemed an unnecessary and trivial restriction and her boldness had been rewarded. She had gotten away with it, and now why shouldn't Adam do the same?

What sort of world might it have been if Eve had

refused the Serpent's offer and had said to him instead, "Let me not be like God. Let me be what I was made to be—let me be a woman"?

But the sin was fatal beyond their worst imaginings. It was *hubris*, a lifting up of the soul in defiance of God, the pride that usurps another's place. It is a damnable kind of pride.

# SEVEN

# The Right Kind of Pride

But there is another kind of pride, one which every man and woman under God ought to cultivate. Isak Dinesen defines it in her beautiful book *Out of Africa*:

"Pride is faith in the idea that God had when he made us. A proud man is conscious of the idea, and aspires to realize it. He does not strive towards a happiness, or comfort, which may be irrelevant to God's idea of him. His success is the idea of God, successfully carried through, and he is in love with his destiny."

I have learned (but slowly, I'm afraid), what it is to be in love with my destiny. Your father learned it much earlier. "Wherever you are," he wrote, "be all there. Live to the hilt every situation you believe to be the will of God." In my judgment (which I trust is not wholly impaired by my being your mother) you have always known this. You have been, almost from birth, not only accepting but exuberant in your acceptance.

"People who have no pride," Dinesen goes on, "are not aware of any idea of God in the making of

26

them, and sometimes they make you doubt that there has ever been much of an idea, or else it has been lost, and who shall find it again? They have got to accept as success what others warrant to be so, and to take their happiness, and even their own selves, at the quotation of the day."

A few women whose vision is grotesquely distorted are trying to redefine for us a woman's "success," and to tell us that our happiness lies not in the idea of God in the making of us but in obliterating that idea altogether. The creation of male and female as complementary opposites has no place in their thinking, and any definition of masculinity and femininity is totally meaningless except with reference to cultural and social expectation. We may alter masculinity and femininity simply by altering the conditioning processes.

You would understand better than some how greatly cultures and societies differ in their expectations of male and female behavior. For the first eight years of your life you lived with South American Indians who drew sharp distinctions between the sexes. They were not always the distinctions we North Americans would draw, but distinctions none the less. Women wore long hair, men wore short. Men ate first, women waited to eat whatever might be left over when the men had finished. Women were the bearers of heavy burdens. Men were not considered physically capable of this work. Both men and women were willing to work for white people, swinging machetes to clear grass and underbrush, and while the women were usually more efficient at this, their wages were lower than the men's even though the hours were the same. Men hunted, women planted. Men used guns (blowguns or shotguns, depending on how "civilized" they were), women made fishnets, pots, hammocks, sieves. Men wove baskets. You as a little foreign girl took your own place among them, learning to catch fish with your hands as the women did, cooking, mashing, chewing and spitting your manioc in order to make *chicha*, and then, before you drank yours, serving the little boys who were your friends. You learned to swing a machete and to build fires and to walk the trails with one foot in front of the other, and you also knew that, like the Indian children, you were not expected to complain.

I can't remember when we first spoke of sex. You grew up knowing about it. When you were hardly out of diapers you helped me to save the life of a baby who was having a hard time being born. It was a breech presentation and the women had already begun the death wail for both mother and child and refused to help me. I needed a warm cloth to wrap around the baby's body to help keep it from trying to breathe too soon, but no one wanted to soil the clothes they had. You ran and brought me one of your own diapers, and then watched in amazement with the others as the baby was born at last, alive and yelling.

You were only three when we went to live with the Aucas, who were naked people and whose conversation was almost exclusively of hunting, spearing, and sex. There was no choice of vocabulary. The

Auca language did not distinguish between a clinical, a nursery, and a gutter vocabulary. There were perfectly straightforward words for organs, functions, and activities, and any everyday conversation might include them, so you learned them, of course. And now you have forgotten all that, along with all the rest of the language you knew, but you remember the people and the life you lived with them there and for that I am glad.

You always carried your dolls in a carrying cloth as Indian mothers did, and as you yourself had been carried. You played house with the Indian children—something they had never thought of doing, but you showed them how to fix a little place in the hollow of a tree root and build a tiny fire in the middle of it, for, after all, the only really essential item in a house in the jungle was a fire. Were you conforming to social pressures in playing such "girl's" games? Surely not. Surely it was because you were born a woman. There was in you a knowledge divinely given on which your imagination, more active than the Indians', went to work.

As you grew older and we came to the States to live, I remember how eagerly you went to school for the first time. You started the fourth grade and in a few days you had caught the rhythm of this new life, so different from the old one, and in what seemed to me a matter of weeks you had grown up. We had talked when you were small about the wonders of being a woman. Once when you were about four you were interviewed on a children's talk show on the radio.

"What are you going to be when you grow up, Valerie?" you were asked (of course!).

"Just want to be a mommie," was your unhesitating reply.

Growing up was very exciting. You could hardly wait, and when the day came at last when you knew you were a woman indeed, you came to tell me about it and your eyes shone.

# EIGHT

# The Weight of Wings

Perspective makes all the difference in the world. If you catch even a glimpse of the divine design (and who can see more than a glimpse of any part of it?) you will be humbled and awed at least. I believe a true understanding of it will also make you grateful. But there are those to whom being a woman is nothing more than an inconvenience, to be suffered because it is unavoidable and to be ignored if at all possible. Their lives are spent pining to be something else. Every creature of God is given something that could be called an inconvenience, I suppose, depending on one's perspective. The elephant and the mouse might each complain about his size, the turtle about his shell, the bird about the weight of his wings. But elephants are not called upon to run behind wainscots, mice will not be found "pacing along as though they have an appointment at the end of the world," turtles have no need to fly nor birds to creep. The special gift and ability of each creature defines its special limitations. And as the bird easily comes to terms with the necessity of bearing wings when it finds that it is, in fact, the wings that bear the bird—up, away from the world, into the sky, into freedom—so the woman who accepts the limitations of womanhood finds in those very limitations her gifts, her special calling—wings, in fact, which bear her up into perfect freedom, into the will of God.

You have heard me tell of Gladys Aylward, the "Small Woman" of China, whom I heard speak many years ago at Prairie Bible Institute in Alberta. She told how when she was a child she had two great sorrows. One, that while all her friends had beautiful golden hair, hers was black. The other, that while her friends were still growing, she stopped. She was about four feet ten inches tall. But when at last she reached the country to which God had called her to be a missionary, she stood on the wharf in Shanghai and looked around at the people to whom He had called her.

"Every single one of them," she said, "had *black hair*. And every single one of them had stopped growing when I did. And I said, 'Lord God, *You know what You're doing!*'"

# NINE

# Single Life—a Gift

What we are is a gift, and, like other gifts, chosen by the Giver alone. We are not presented with an array of options: What would you like to be? How tall? What color? What temperament would you prefer? Which parents will you choose as forebears?

So you are a woman, chosen from the foundation of the world, given to parents who had asked for a son (and only God knows how often and how profoundly I have thanked Him that that ignorant prayer was denied). And before you were twenty you had given your heart to the man who is to be your husband, so you have not really known what it is to be a single woman. You have not been asked to struggle with that question. Relatively few women have to, for most women marry. And of those who marry, 90 percent do so before the age of twenty-one, which means that they have not known what it is to be a single woman in the world. They have probably lived with and been provided for by their parents most of their lives. Many have been in college until the time of their marriage, as you will have been, and hence have had their time mapped out for them. No major decisions will ever have been entirely up to them.

I have told you a little of my own perplexity about this issue when I was a college student, for I believed God was calling me to be a missionary and quite possibly a single one. I wanted to be a missionary, but I did not want to be a single one. It seemed that I was to go to Africa, and the only man I had any interest in was on his way to South America, the one place I had been quite certain I would never go.

There came a day, only a week before I graduated, when that man and I had a talk about marriage and the directions in which God seemed to be leading us, and I remember his telling me then that St. Paul regarded single life as a gift. Well, I thought wryly, St. Paul did have some bizarre ideas, and was certainly not to be taken too seriously in his views on marriage. What did he know about marriage? He was single because he liked being single and I was suspicious of a man like that. (It has since occurred to me that we have no evidence that Paul had never been married.)

But having now spent more than forty-one years single, I have learned that it is indeed a gift. Not one I would choose. Not one many women would choose. But we do not choose gifts, remember? We are given them by a divine Giver who knows the end from the beginning, and wants above all else to give us the gift of Himself. It is within the sphere of the circumstances He chooses for us—single, married, widowed—that we receive Him. It is there and nowhere else that He makes Himself known to us. It is there we are allowed to serve Him.

In 1 Corinthians 7 Paul says it is best for each man to have his own wife, and for each woman to have her own husband, "because of the temptation to immorality." Then he says almost immediately, "I wish that all were as I myself am. But each has his own special gift from God, one of one kind and one of another. To the unmarried and the widows I say that it is well for them to remain single as I do. But if they cannot exercise self-control, they should marry. For it is better to marry than to be aflame with passion."

For the next five years after my graduation, until I married him, that young man and I waited on God, prayed, searched the Scriptures, corresponded, and, on very widely-spaced occasions, were able to talk about these matters. Was Paul setting the single life above marriage? It had certainly seemed so. He spoke of the weakness which could not resist temptation, and of the hindrances to service for God which marriage would inevitably bring. He reminded the Corinthians of the "impending distress" which would make it unwise for a person to seek to change his marital status in any way. He said that the man who marries his betrothed does well but the man who refrains from marriage does *better*. A widow, in Paul's judgment, is *happier* if she does not remarry, and he thought that he had the Spirit of God in this.

No wonder we were confused, and no wonder that a man of your father's determination should ponder long and earnestly the apparent contradictions in this hard chapter. He longed for the "better" and "happier" way. He was determined to prove God's strength and grace sufficient to overcome the ordinary weakness of a man's flesh. He knew his own great attraction for women. He was determined also to serve the Lord without entanglements. But the time came when marriage was for him a clear command, and he knew then that it was a gift, given by the same Giver who gives to some the special gift of being single. "Let every one lead the life which the Lord has assigned to him," Paul wrote.

To a young man who was vacillating on the question of marriage Martin Luther wrote:

"Chastity is not in our power, as little as are God's other wonders and graces. But we are all made for marriage as our bodies show and as the Scriptures state in Genesis 2. 'It is not good that man should be alone; I will make him a help meet for him.'

"I fancy that human fear and timidity stand in your way. It is said that it takes a bold man to venture to take a wife. What you need above all else, then, is to be encouraged, admonished, urged, incited, and made bold. Why should you delay, my dear and reverend sir, and continue to weigh the matter in your mind? It must, it should, and will happen in any case. Stop thinking about it and go to it right merrily. Your body demands it, God wills it, and drives you to it. There is nothing that you can do about it . . . It is best to comply with all our senses as soon as possible and give ourselves to God's Word and work in whatever He wishes us to do.

"Let us not try to fly higher and be better than

Abraham, David, Isaiah, Peter, Paul and all the patriarchs, prophets, and apostles, as well as many holy martyrs and bishops, all of whom knew that they were created by God as men, were not ashamed to be and be thought men, conducted themselves accordingly, and did not remain alone. Whoever is ashamed of marriage is also ashamed of being a man or being thought a man, or else he thinks that he can make himself better than God made him."

# TEN

# *One Day at a Time*

A couple of years ago I was talking to a group of students about the single life and remarked that I considered myself, as a widow, a thousand times better off than a woman who had never been married. A girl in the group challenged this statement. Why in the world did I think I was better off? Well, quite simply, I answered, because I thought it was better to have loved and lost than never to have loved at all. Why? she wanted to know again. I admitted that this was purely a matter of opinion, and if in her opinion she was better off than I, far be it from me to attempt to change her mind.

Recently I met for the first time a woman who told me she is single by choice. I have met other women who had chances to marry men they did not want to marry, but who would still have liked to marry the "right" one. The lady I met recently was the first to tell me she had chosen the single life.

To the rude questions often asked single ladies one of my acquaintance answers that she is "single for a perfectly good reason that isn't public property."

One lady in her sixties still declares that she does not have what Paul calls the gift of single life. She has lived these sixty years without it for God has assured her, she assures me, that He has a husband for her somewhere. She has only to wait for him to appear. She may be right that God has a husband for her. I think she's wrong in saying she hasn't the gift of single life. She has had it all her life. God may yet give her the gift of marriage, for many of His gifts may be given for only a part of a lifetime. I know of three Christians who had for a short time the gift of healing other people and then it was withdrawn. Why should He not give single life for most of a lifetime and then give marriage? Or may He not give marriage and then, sometimes early in life, widowhood?

The truth is that none of us knows the will of God for his life. I say *for his life*—for the promise is "as thou goest step by step I will open up the way before thee." He gives us enough light for today, enough strength for one day at a time, enough manna, our "daily" bread. And the life of faith is a journey from Point A to Point B, from Point B to Point C, as the people of Israel "set out and encamped in Oboth. And they set out from Oboth and encamped at Iyeabarim, in the wilderness . . . From there they set out and encamped on the other side of the Arnon . . . and from there they continued to Beer . . . and from the wilderness they went on to Mattanah, and from Mattanah to Nahaliel, and from Nahaliel to Bamoth, and from Bamoth to the valley lying in the region of Moab."

So far as we know, nothing happened in these places. Oboth, Iyeabarim, Arnon, Beer, Mattanah, Nahaliel, Bamoth mean nothing to us. That immense crowd just kept moving. They traveled and they stopped and they made camp and packed up again and traveled some more and made another camp. They complained. There were so many complaints that even Moses, who was a very meek man, could hardly stand the sight of these whom God had called him to lead. But all the time God was with them, leading them, protecting them, hearing their cries, goading and guiding them, knowing where they were going and what His purposes were for them and He never left them.

It is not difficult when you read the whole story of God's deliverance of Israel to see how each separate incident fits into a pattern for good. We have perspective that those miserable wanderers didn't have. But it should help us to trust their God. The stages of their journey, dull and eventless as most of them were, were each a necessary part of the movement toward the fulfillment of the promise.

Single life may be only a stage of a life's journey, but even a stage is a gift. God may replace it with another gift, but the receiver accepts His gifts with thanksgiving. *This* gift for *this* day. The life of faith is lived one day at a time, and it has to be *lived*—not always looked forward to as though the "real" living were around the next corner. It is today for which we are responsible. God still owns tomorrow.

# ELEVEN

# Trust for Separation

But you are about to be married. For you surely the "real living" seems to be around the corner, and it is natural and right that you should anticipate that wonderful day which will begin a whole new kind of life for you. Yet you, too, as much as a single woman who had no visible prospects, have to live the life of faith. You understand the calling of your sexuality, to be a woman in fellowship with all other women and all men. You are not a woman only in relation to Walt. If this were so, of course, single women would be deprived of the meaning of their sexuality. Their happiness and fulfillment would lie in sublimation to the point of denial of that which distinguishes them from men. This is not the truth of Scripture. Scripture teaches that the distinctions established by creation are each a part of the Design, each necessary and irreplaceable. I know no better word than *called*. It is an astounding thing to know ourselves individually called. A call comes to us as women, but it comes to us as individual women also, and it is as individual women that we must answer.

There have been long weeks of separation from

Walt when you did things you wanted achingly for him to share. His graduation came on a day when it was impossible for you to be present and you had to miss it. His ordination to the ministry took place while you were in England. He began his preaching without you, and those experiences can never be recovered or relived.

I remember how it was. Your father (not my fiancé yet) made the three-week voyage by sea from San Pedro, California, to Ecuador, stopping at fascinating ports along the way, from which he sent me fascinating letters. He began his study of Spanish in Quito without me. He made his first trip to the jungle where he was later to work. He had his first opportunity to do medical work, his first crack at an unwritten language—all of these were things I myself longed to do, and longed desperately to do with him. "Let not our longing slay the appetite of our living," he wrote to me, and those words have helped me very often since. We accept and thank God for what is given, not allowing the *not-given* to spoil it.

This is the call. This is the order of our lives. There is nothing haphazard about them. We can commit them to God, and accept them from Him. This is part of what Walt meant by "Ma'am, I'm a Calvinist!"

# TWELVE

# Self-Discipline and Order

There is a hymn by John Greenleaf Whittier which says:

> Drop Thy still dews of quietness
> Till all our strivings cease.
> Take from our souls the strain and stress,
> And let our ordered lives confess
> The beauty of Thy peace.

We are the creatures of a great Master-Designer, and His ordering of our lives is sure and certain, yet many people live without any visible order or peace or serenity. The way we live ought to manifest the truth of what we believe. A messy life speaks of a messy—an incoherent—faith.

It is something we have worked on for a long time, haven't we, Val, this matter of order? It means self-discipline. "If ye continue in my words, then are ye my disciples indeed and ye shall know the truth and the truth shall make you free." Freedom begins way back. It begins not with doing what you want but with doing what you ought—that is, with discipline. With "continuing in the word." To be a disciple means to be disciplined. And we have worked at that, haven't we? From the day you were born, almost, I tried to teach you that the word I spoke was the word I meant. It was to be taken seriously, to be lived by, in your child-life. How shall we learn to believe and obey God if we have not been taught from earliest childhood to believe and obey the ones He puts over us? A child has to know first of all and beyond any shadow of doubt that the word spoken will be the word carried out. Threats ("If you don't do this, you'll be spanked") or promises ("If you pick up all your toys you'll get a popsicle")—if not carried through are ruinous to a child's morality. Failure to fulfill threats and promises trains a child to discount what is said. It trains him to lie. The parents are not to be trusted, therefore they need not be obeyed, therefore no authority is trustworthy or need be obeyed. Obedience is optional, depending on convenience or inclination or obvious reward.

God has not so taught us. "In the beginning was the Word, and the Word was with God, and the Word was God." "He that heareth my Word and doeth it, he it is that loveth me." "If ye love me, keep my commandments." And "His commandments are not grievous."

When you were small there were always Indians around us, and I had many things on my mind in the running of a jungle mission station. I was sometimes tempted to pay little attention to your small needs. You knew it at once. You knew whether it was an opportune time to get away with something. You would try it, and my preoccupied, "Val, leave that alone," you would ignore. You knew you could safely ignore it because my attention had already turned back to the thing at hand. I learned very soon that I had to give my full attention to you when I spoke. I do not mean that I gave you my full attention twenty-four hours of the day. I see mothers who very nearly accomplish this and they do it to the destruction of their poor smothered, harried children. I mean that when a matter needs the mother's attention it must get her full attention for that moment. I had to turn from my work and turn to you.

Your eyes would open wide when I stopped what I was doing and looked at you. Slowly, slowly, your hand would drop when I said your name. In the moment of pause and silence you assessed my seriousness. Either I meant it or I did not, and there was no dissimulating with you. You knew which it was and acted accordingly.

My job is over now. You are a woman, God's woman, autonomous before Him. But His disciplining of you is far from finished. If you love Him, you'll do what He says. And there can be no question as to whether He means it if only you will look at His face, be silent long enough to hear what He says. "He calls his own sheep by name." It was when Mary heard her name that she knew her Master in the garden after His resurrection. "Master!" she cried, in recognition of His lordship over her.

The way you keep your house, the way you organize your time, the care you take in your personal appearance, the things you spend your money on all speak loudly about what you believe. "The beauty of Thy peace" shines forth in an ordered life. A disordered life speaks loudly of disorder in the soul.

# THIRTEEN

# Whose Battle?

Last night before I went to bed I looked out across the harbor and saw that one of the boats was lit up. Work must have been going on, for this morning the boat is piled high with lobster pots on the deck, and although it is nearly noon she still lies anchored, swinging gently in the wind. I wonder when the fisherman will take her out to sea to set his pots? Perhaps the wind is too strong.

Three purple finches, a song sparrow, and a robin are busy on the front lawn. The finches are looking for the puddle where they have been bathing regularly. It has dried up in the sun. The song sparrow finds seeds in the grass. The robin, a sleek, handsome male, cocks his head to listen (is it true that they can really hear worms crawling?) then dives headfirst into the ground, comes up with a worm which he tugs and tugs and finally wrenches free and swallows. A bob-white repeats his name again and again in the thicket behind the house. There are more wild roses blooming this morning on the rail fence across the road—vivid pink and white.

You would love it here, I know, for you have

always loved the sun and the outdoors. But you have it in you, too, I am sure, to love London. I have been there only once, but I was captivated and held by the solidity of the place and by what I can only call a great, noble elegance. There it stands, still London after so many centuries, after the unimaginable bombing of World War II, still a strong, proud city. I felt as though I had known it centuries ago and was glad to find it again. Perhaps today it is cold and rainy there, while the sun shines brilliantly here.

I have just received in the mail a magazine containing several pieces on the ordination of women. The authors take a less serious view of the Creation story than I do, and base most of their arguments on the competence of women to do the job of a priest or a minister. This is a pretty convincing argument at first glance. The church needs ministers, women make good ones, why not let women be ordained? Fish swim, birds fly, men trap lobsters, robins yank worms out of their safe underground tunnels, cities rise, civilization moves ahead—isn't it all a part of the great rhythm and harmony of things? I believe the Lord is in charge. I have to believe that even when I think of what the wooden pots mean to the lobsters themselves, and of what the robin's deadly beak means to the hard-working worm, and of the uncalculated pain and sin of London, or the many places in that city where it is not at all noble or elegant.

The universe moves at the command of God, and men and women are at all times under that command, but, distinct from robins and lobsters, they have been given the power to disobey. They are capable of doing a great many things they are not supposed to do. The ability to do them is not a command to do them. It is not even permission. This simple fact, so obvious in the physical realm (we know perfectly well we're not supposed to smash other people in the face, capable and eager to do so though we may sometimes be), is easily obscured in the intellectual and spiritual realms. We discern in ourselves certain propensities or even gifts and, without thought for possible restrictions which may be placed upon their use, start wielding them. The results may be far more destructive than smashing somebody in the face. Men and women who have used their minds, their talents, and their genius to move multitudes to evil have used the minds, talents, and genius given to them by their Creator. But they have not asked what God has commanded. They have not offered themselves first to Him, trusting His direction for their proper sphere of operation.

So the question of ordination hinges on far more than competence. It cannot be decided on the basis of the church's need or an individual's urge or any of the sociological or humanistic arguments put forth by those who seek to liberate. It has to do with things vastly more fundamental and permanent, and the meaning of womanhood is one of these things.

We have something to respond to, something that directs and calls and holds us, and it is in obedience to the command that we will find our full freedom.

# FOURTEEN

# Freedom through Discipline

As I sit here in the window of this cottage I can see a sailboat skimming silently along the horizon. It is a beautiful image of freedom. But the freedom of the sailboat to move so swiftly and beautifully is the result of obedience to laws. The builder of the boat had to know the proper ratio of beam to keel and mast. The one who sails the boat obeys the rules of sailing. A ship tacking against the wind moves deviously, but when she runs with a strong tide or a following wind she takes to herself the power of tide and wind and they become her own. She is doing the thing she was made for. She is free not by disobeying the rules but by obeying them.

Modern highways are often called freeways, but how much freedom of movement would there be if each driver were encouraged to choose any lane, any speed, any direction that happened to appeal to his fancy at the moment?

I noticed on Boston Common a sign saying "Please," which the public was expected to understand was short for "Please keep off the grass." Almost everybody had obeyed that sign and that's why there was still some grass. But there were a few people sitting on the grass in defiance of the sign. Their freedom to sit on grass instead of on bare dirt was dependent on the majority's having denied themselves the privilege. The majority had made the choice to allow grass to grow. This choice meant restriction, a willingness to limit themselves to the walks. It meant *not* doing what they wanted to do in order to have something they wanted more. The freedom of the few was bought at the sacrifice of the many.

You and I have talked about college students' idea of freedom in dormitories. They don't want lights-out rules or coming-in rules or quiet rules. Consequently, this freedom of theirs to keep the lights on till all hours, to stay out most of the night, and to play records at three A.M. means that there's no freedom to sleep, there's not even the freedom to study, which means that students are no longer free to be students, the very thing they've come to college and paid fifteen thousand dollars to be.

This is the crux of the question of liberty and liberation. Does it mean casting off all restrictions? (Could a ship sail without them?) Does it mean doing what we feel like doing and not doing what we don't? It means discipline. It means doing the thing we were meant for. What is it to which we are called, we women under God?

# FIFTEEN

# God Sets No Traps

We are called to be women. The fact that I am a woman does not make me a different kind of Christian, but the fact that I am a Christian does make me a different kind of woman. For I have accepted God's idea of me, and my whole life is an offering back to Him of all that I am and all that He wants me to be.

Ruth Benedict, one of the first women to attain recognition as a major social scientist, wrote in her journal in 1912: "To me it seems a very terrible thing to be a woman. There is one crown which perhaps is worth it all—a great love, a quiet home, and children. [Her childless marriage to Stanley Benedict ended in divorce.] We all know that is all that is worthwhile, and we must peg away, showing off our wares on the market if we have money, or manufacturing careers for ourselves if we haven't. We have not the motive to prepare ourselves for a 'lifework' of teaching, of social work—we know that we would lay it down with hallelujah in the height of our success, to make a home for the right man. And all the time in the background of our consciousness rings the warning that perhaps the right man will never come. A great love is given to very few. Perhaps this makeshift time-filler of a job *is* our lifework after all."

Mrs. Benedict has expressed candidly what thousands of career women must surely feel, but today there are few who would have the courage to admit to such feelings, when the career woman is thought by many to be somehow superior to the woman whose occupation is listed merely as "housewife." Any nine-to-five job, no matter how routine, monotonous, or boring, is elevated by the feminists to higher status than being a wife and mother, as though the wife and mother's work were more demeaning, more boring, less creative and exciting, or allowed less latitude for one's imagination than being a lawyer or fitting parts on an assembly line. (Granted, feminists nearly always pit prestige jobs rather than assembly-line jobs against housework, ignoring the fact that few of the women they would like to "liberate" would end up in prestige jobs.)

Recently I found a notice in the newspaper of new job expectations for women joining the Army. No longer are they limited to being secretaries or nurses or assistants to men. In at least one Army training center they have been elevated to parachute-packing. Parachute packing!

I'm afraid it's a case of the grass's being greener on the other side of the fence. How many of them have had a fair chance to compare?

For the Christian woman, however, whether she is married or single, there is the call to serve. A news magazine recently reported an adult course offered in "Assertive Behavior," which, according to the descriptions of sample situations, amounted to a course in boorishness. One lesson, for example, encouraged women to break free from the "compassion trap." In response to this article a reader wrote, "I cannot understand why a woman would object to being a part of the 'compassion trap'—the need to serve others and provide tenderness and compassion at all times. What this society needs is more emphasis on the need to serve others, and provide tenderness, compassion, cooperation and love."

But God has set no traps for us. Quite the contrary. He has summoned us to the only true and full freedom. The woman who defines her liberation as doing what she wants, or not doing what she doesn't want, is, in the first place, evading responsibility. Evasion of responsibility is the mark of immaturity. The Women's Liberation Movement is characterized, it appears, by this very immaturity. While telling themselves that they've come a long way, that they are actually coming of age, they have retreated to a partial humanity, one which refuses to acknowledge the vast significance of the sexual differentiation. (I do not say that they always ignore sexual differentiation itself, but that the *significance* of it escapes them entirely.) And the woman who ignores that fundamental truth ironically misses the very thing she has set out to find. By refusing to fulfill the whole vocation of womanhood she settles for a caricature, a pseudo-personhood.

# A *Paradoxical Principle*

You and I have known, either personally or through their writings, some great single women whose lives were rich and fruitful because they understood a paradoxical spiritual principle: "If you pour yourself out for the hungry and satisfy the desire of the afflicted, then shall your light rise in the darkness and your gloom be as the noonday. And the Lord will guide you continually, and satisfy your desire with good things, and make your bones strong; and you shall be like a watered garden, like a spring of water, whose waters fail not. And your ancient ruins shall be rebuilt; you shall raise up the foundations of many generations; you shall be called the repairer of the breach, the restorer of streets to dwell in" (or, instead of "streets to dwell in" another translation says "paths leading home").

Here, I think, lies the answer to the barrenness of a single life, or of a life that might otherwise be selfish or lonely. It is the answer, I have found, to depression as well. You yourself will be given light in exchange for pouring yourself out for the hungry; you yourself will get guidance, the satisfaction of your longings, and strength, when you "pour your-self out," when you make the satisfaction of some-body else's desire your own concern; you yourself will be a source of refreshment, a builder, a leader into healing and rest at a time when things around you seem to have crumbled.

Amy Carmichael of India never married, though there are faint hints in her biography that she had had to make the choice and that it was an extremely painful thing for her to take up a cross which meant leaving a man forever. But her life was a watered garden, to the hundreds of Indian children who came under her care, and to the thousands who read her books.

Katherine Morgan of Colombia, a widow ever since her four girls were small, has shown us by her exuberance and humor, by her generous warm heart and her awesome energy, the strength that comes in giving a life up utterly for the good of others. Her house is full of people who need her. She drives a pick-up truck all over the city of Pasto doing things for people who can't do for themselves. She goes to the jungle by muleback or canoe or on foot to minister to people far from other sources of help. She comes to see us when she is in the States and ministers to us though she is not conscious of ministering. Our house is blessed and we ourselves are cheered and fortified because she has been here. She's always breathless—she talks so fast she has to pronounce half her sentences on the intake. She's always funny, and has us in tears of laughter as she impersonates a character in a story. I have often teased her for saying, "Life is too short" when I have wanted her to do something I thought she ought to do, but what it boils down to is that life is too short to bother about herself. She's never too busy to bother about the rest of us.

You are not to live a single life, but the life of a minister's wife will give ample scope to prove the principle set forth in Isaiah's words. You will be pouring yourself out for the hungry and it will be assumed that you are a spring of water whose waters fail not and there will be times when you are tired of that pouring out. Your step-father told of a lady who came to him distraught with all that was expected of her. "I work my fingers to the bone for this church and what kind of thanks do I get?" she wailed. "Well," he said, "what kind of thanks did you expect?"

St. Ignatius of Loyola prayed, "Teach us, Good Lord, to serve Thee as Thou deservest; to give and not to count the cost; to fight and not to heed the wounds; to toil and not to seek for rest; to labor and not to ask for any reward save that of knowing that we do Thy will. Through Jesus Christ our Lord."

# SEVENTEEN

# Masculine and Feminine

Do the women's liberationists want to be liberated from being women? No, they would say, they want to be liberated from society's stereotypes of what women are supposed to be. There are, according to their theorists, no fundamental differences between men and women. It is all a matter of conditioning. Some very interesting facts have been uncovered by scientists which feminists will have to treat very gingerly for they show that it is not merely society which determines how the sexes will behave. There are strong biological reasons (a matter of hormones) why the male has always dominated and will continue to dominate in every society. The idea of matriarchy is mythical, I've learned, for not one that can be documented has ever existed. Doesn't it seem strange that male dominance has been universal if it's purely social conditioning? One would expect to see at least a few examples of societies where women rather than men held the positions of highest status. (The existence of reigning queens proves nothing, since they have their position by heritage, not by achievement, choice, or election.)

Isn't it really much easier to believe that the feelings of men and women throughout history bear a direct relationship to some innate prerequisite? For a scientist that prerequisite may be biological and/or emotional (the least suggestion that there might be an emotional as well as a physical difference between males and females is for some women horrifying) but for you and me the prerequisite lies further back.

It was God who made us different, and He did it on purpose. Recent scientific research is illuminating, and as has happened before, corroborates ancient truth which mankind has always recognized. God created male and female, the male to call forth, to lead, initiate and rule, and the female to respond, follow, adapt, submit. Even if we held to a different theory of origin the physical structure of the female would tell us that woman was made to receive, to bear, to be acted upon, to complement, to nourish.

Last year you audited a course in seminary which required you to write a paper defining masculinity and femininity. The class agreed that this was the most difficult assignment of the semester, but the one who came closest to a definition was Kathy Kristy who wrote:

"Creation has as one of its fundamental themes the pattern of rule and submission. Power and passivity, ebb and flow, generativity and receptivity are but a few of the ways that these paired polarities have been described. The Chinese called them *yin* and *yang* and made the symbol of their religion a graphic representation of their interaction. Even the physical realm is founded on and held together by the positive and negative attraction of atomic particles. Everywhere the universe displays its division into pairs of interlocking opposites. . .

"We know that this order of rule and submission is descended from the nature of God Himself. Within the Godhead there is both the just and legitimate authority of the Father and the willing and joyful submission of the Son. From the union of the Father and the Son proceeds a third personality, the Holy Spirit. He proceeds from them not as a child proceeds from the union of a man and a woman, but rather as the personality of a marriage proceeds from the one flesh which is established from the union of two separate personalities.

"Here, in the reflection of the nature of the Trinity in the institution of marriage is the key to the definition of masculinity and femininity. The image of God could not be fully reflected without the elements of rule, submission, and union."

There is a fundamental and to me quite puzzling omission in most "feminist" discussion—the failure to talk at all about femininity. Perhaps it is because the elements of rule, submission, and union are part and parcel of femininity itself and of far more lasting and universal importance than any culturally defined notion. To get at this the place to start, obviously, is the body itself.

A human being comprises body, mind, and spirit. Any doctor will attest to the effect the mind may have on the body. Any psychiatrist knows that his patient's psychological problems may have physical effects. Any minister admits that what appears to be a spiritual issue may turn out to have physical and mental dimensions as well. No one can define the boundaries of mind, body, and spirit. Yet we are asked to assume nowadays that sexuality, most potent and undeniable of all human characteristics, is a purely physical matter with no metaphysical significance whatever.

Some early heresies which plagued the Church urged Christians to bypass matter. Some said it was in and of itself only evil. Some denied even its reality. Some appealed to the spiritual nature of man as alone worthy of attention—the body was to be ignored altogether. But this is a dangerous business, this departmentalizing. The Bible tells us to bring all—body, mind, spirit—under obedience.

Yours is the body of a woman. What does it signify? Is there invisible meaning in its visible signs—the softness, the smoothness, the lighter bone and muscle structure, the breasts, the womb? Are they utterly unrelated to what you yourself are? Isn't your identity intimately bound up with these material forms? Does the idea of you—Valerie— contain the idea of, let's say, "strapping" or "husky?" How can we bypass matter in our search for understanding the personality? There is a strange unreality in those who would do so, an unwillingness to deal with the most obvious facts of all.

Every normal woman is equipped to be a mother. Certainly not every woman in the world is destined to make use of the physical equipment but surely motherhood, in a deeper sense, is the essence of womanhood. The body of every normal woman prepares itself repeatedly to receive and to bear. Motherhood requires self-giving, sacrifice, suffering. It is a going down into death in order to give life, a great human analogy of a great spiritual principle (Paul wrote, "Death worketh in us but life in you"). Womanhood is a call. It is a vocation to which we respond under God, glad if it means the literal bearing of children, thankful as well for all that it means in a much wider sense, that in which every woman, married or single, fruitful or barren, may participate—the unconditional response exemplified for all time in Mary the virgin, and the willingness to enter into suffering, to receive, to carry, to give life, to nurture and to care for others. The strength to answer this call is given us as we look up toward the Love that created us, remembering that it was that Love that first, most literally, *imagined* sexuality, that made us at the very beginning real men and real women. As we conform to that Love's demands we shall become more humble, more dependent—on Him and on one another—and even (dare I say it?) more splendid.

# EIGHTEEN

# *The Soul Is Feminine*

It is still early morning as I sit down to my typewriter, although I have been up to the Coast Guard Station on my bicycle and seen thirty-one rabbits and two deer and looked through the pay telescope at the rusted hulk of the tanker Pendleton which was wrecked in 1952. The tide is low. The clam diggers are out on the salt flats across the harbor with their rakes, and a schooner has just been towed by. Yesterday's strong wind has subsided and the harbor is calm, the air still and warm.

Wind, weather, and tide fulfill His word. It is a calming, steadying thing to know that there is a word for us as well. Psalm 144:12 says, "May our daughters be like corner pillars cut for the structure of a palace." Pillars uphold and support. This is a woman's place, and all of us need to know what our place is and to be put in it. The command of God puts us there where we belong. We know our "creatureliness," our dependence. If there is a command for us we know we are recognized. We know that we fit into God's universe, we know our relation to the rest of mankind, to the family, and, if we have one, to a husband. Meekness, I believe, is the recognition of that place. Moses, the Bible tells us, was a "very meek man." I don't think of him at all as meek in the popular sense—timid, self-abnegating, colorless. Far from it. But to be meek is to have a sane and proper estimate of one's place in the scheme of things. It is a sense of proportion.

According as a pillar is cut and shaped to fit into a particular place and carry a specified weight, it is by that cutting and shaping differentiated and limited. It is the very differentiation and limitation that that pillar has to offer. So with us. We've been cut to a certain size and shape to fulfill a certain function. It is this, not that. It is a woman's offering, not a man's, that we have to give.

Mary is the archetype of human self-giving. When told of the awesome privilege which was to be hers as the mother of the Most High her response was total acceptance. "Behold the handmaid of the Lord. Be it unto me according to Thy word." She might have hesitated because she didn't want to go through life being known only as somebody's mother. She might have had her own dreams of fulfillment. But she embraced at once the will of God. Her "Be it unto me" ought to be the response of every man or woman to that will, and it is in this sense that the soul and the Church have been seen throughout Christian history as female before God, for it is the nature of the woman to submit.

# Is Submission Stifling?

Does a submissive woman do nothing else but submit? It is too bad that the issues raised by those
called liberationists have led to the making of false
antitheses. It is an old political tactic and seems at
first to strengthen the case for one side against the
other, but ultimately it is self-destructive. The mail
has just come, bringing a letter which illustrates
this confusion.

You were present when I spoke recently to the
honor society in your college on "A Christian View
of Liberation." The college forwarded to me the
protest of an alumna:

"To invite a speaker to tell the women who have
just been chosen as the most academically gifted in
the entire graduating class that their highest fulfillment is to be found in subjecting themselves to a
man in marriage is incredible in this day and age. It
would have been unthinkable even a century ago!
Why is this college educating women if their primary calling is to be motherhood? Intellectual
women in the Christian world have a difficult
enough time without adding insult to injury. They

need encouragement, not stifling. I have always personally found (the speaker's) actual accomplishments a real inspiration but when her rhetoric so completely contradicts that, she makes an ambiguous role model at best for those of us who have traveled the road a ways [sic]. For college graduates just embarking on that road, she could be seriously confusing."

The writer of this letter withheld her usual annual contribution in protest, and added that she felt the choice of a speaker was "particularly inappropriate."

I had never thought of myself as "an ambiguous role model." I guess I had never thought of myself as any sort of role model. Does my rhetoric contradict my accomplishments? Is there anything in what I say that stifles "intellectual women in the Christian world"?

I've tried to think these charges through. I suppose I am an "ambiguous role model" if a mother is not supposed to write books, or if a wife who is submissive would never be asked to speak on a college platform, or if no college graduate ought to love housework.

Is it my rhetoric or is it perhaps the rhetoric of this lady herself (who has written and spoken on the equality of the sexes) which contradicts my "accomplishments"? If I have said that a woman's highest fulfillment is to be found in subjecting herself to a man in marriage, I meant, of course, the woman to whom God has given the gift of marriage. Her highest fulfillment will be found in obedience to that calling. I who have had that gift, as well as the gift of being your mother, have no difficulty whatever in saying that my deepest sense of "fulfillment," my highest human joys, have been found in being a wife and mother.

This is not to deny or belittle the other gifts God has given. I have been called to be a missionary and to write, but surely there is nothing incompatible with such tasks and acknowledgement of the fundamental fact that woman was made for man. That wasn't my idea, after all—I got it all out of the Book!

The "intellectual" women who feel stifled by what I say have not yet understood the biblical meaning of freedom. God's service is, as our Prayer Book says, "perfect freedom."

The lady's idea that mothers do not need a college education floors me. What, she asks, is your college educating women for? Surely it is to *draw out* (the root meaning of the word *educate*) the gifts God has given, whatever they may be. Surely I did not send you to college on the assumption that you would not marry. A Christian liberal education will make you a better wife and mother, I'm convinced, if that is God's will for you. If you were called to be a tax collector or a philosopher I should likewise want you to have that kind of education.

# *Twenty Questions*

It is a long way from the recognition of a Logos, an Eternal Word who speaks and under whom we live, to the specific destiny to which you yourself as an individual woman are called. Yet the God who controls the wheeling galaxies and who spoke before the foundation of the world must be the God who holds the smallest circumstance of your life in His hands. We are encompassed on all sides by the Almighty. "His tender mercies are *over* all His works," "steadfast love *surrounds* him who trusts in the Lord," and "*underneath* are the Everlasting Arms." Over, around, underneath. We are enfolded. Can you think of a safer place to be? Yet God does not coerce us into doing His will. He has given us free choice, and it is in this freedom that you and Walt have chosen to marry. You have answered the questions I posed for you a year ago when you were trying to define and sort out your feelings. (They were pretty clear to me when I saw your radiant face as you ran to the car from the post office, waving a letter from him.)

Here are the questions:

1) Is this the man you want to spend the rest of your life with? That's every day of every week of every month of every year from now till one of you dies.

2) Is he:

punctual or habitually late?

orderly or disorderly?

a reader or a TV watcher?

an outdoor man or an indoor man?

3) Does he:

like your family?

treat you as you think a woman ought to be treated?

have men friends?

have approximately the same education you have?

like the kind of food you like to cook?

come from a home similar to yours?

like your friends?

like to entertain, and would you be proud to have him as host at the other end of the table?

laugh at the same jokes you do?

4) Can you agree on:

sex?

in-laws?

children and their training?

money?

your respective roles in the home?

You have faced all these questions and the important areas of concern that they point to. Let me assure you that I've known happy couples of which one is an indoor person and the other an outdoor one, or one punctual and the other late, but it requires particular grace, and it's just as well to consider in advance whether or not you think it's going to be worth it. Later, when you're up against it, remind yourself that it's worth it!

You know that I do not insist that every question under 3) must be answered Yes if your marriage is to be a success. And of course agreement in the matters of 4) can only be in principle until you've had the chance to work on them as husband and wife. There is no practice session for these. Deep, underlying principles will determine your handling of these things, and you must thoroughly agree on these before you agree to marry a man. This is why I did not include religion on the list. "Religion" is not simply one of many matters to be debated about on a par with child-training and the treatment of in-laws. It will determine the child-training and how you treat your in-laws. It is the foundation of your life. As soon as you begin discussing the things on the list you will be discussing religion, for "all our problems are theological ones."

How can you possibly agree on sex unless you agree on morality? If morality is merely a matter of taste or community tolerance its foundation constantly shifts. If it has the Word as its foundation it's unshakable.

How can you agree on in-laws if you aren't acquainted with the law of love in 1 Corinthians 13?

Whether and when to have children and how to train them are decisions which must be made under God.

How you handle your money will depend on whose it is first (God's or yours?) and what is important to you.

It is mutual commitment to a common belief that is the only solid base for lasting communion, in marriage or in any other fellowship. Anything less will not stand the test of living.

# TWENTY-ONE

# *A Choice Is a Limitation*

Your most recent letter to me, written just after Walt had left you, said, "Oh, Mama, it gets better and better!" You spoke of the utter peace and contentment you know when you are with him. We can believe that God has answered our prayers—mine of years' standing, "Keep her from and for the man she is to marry," ("from" meaning until His chosen time, that you would not hurry ahead of His will)—and yours to be guided to the man of His choice.

And so you wear his ring. Tertullian alludes to the ancient custom of wearing a gold ring on the fourth finger because it was believed that a vein ran from that finger directly to the heart. A woman was allowed to wear gold only there, in promise of marriage. In the medieval service the wedding ring was placed first on the thumb, "in the name of the Father," then on the index finger, "in the name of the Son," on the third finger, "in the name of the Holy Ghost," and on the fourth finger with the Amen.

When the wedding ring is put on your finger you

will have finally sealed your choice. It is this man, and this one alone, whom you have chosen for "as long as ye both shall live." There have been many revisions and improvisations in modern weddings, some of them made in the belief that words written by the bride and groom themselves are by that very fact to be preferred above old words written by somebody who knew how to write, because they are more "sincere" or "meaningful" or "honest," as though the repetition of others' words, probably clearer and more beautiful words than most of us could ever have written, cannot possibly be truthful. In one of these improvisations the phrase has been changed from "as long as ye both shall live" to "as long as we both shall love." This cuts the heart out of the deepest meaning of the wedding. It is a vow you are making before God and before witnesses, a vow you will by God's grace keep, which does not depend on your moods or feelings or "how things turn out." As others have said, love does not preserve the marriage, the marriage preserves love.

When you make a choice, you accept the limitations of that choice. To accept limitation requires maturity. The child has not yet learned that it can't have everything. What it sees it wants. What it does not get it screams for. It has to grow up to realize that saying Yes to happiness often means saying No to yourself.

Remember Dinesen's proud man: "He does not strive toward a happiness or comfort which may be irrelevant to God's idea of him." To choose to do this is to choose not to do a thousand other things. Those who made themselves eunuchs for the kingdom of God, of whom Jesus speaks in Matthew 19:12, had to accept the radical limitations which being a eunuch imposed. Those who marry, Paul said, will have trouble in the flesh. Perhaps he felt that that statement was beyond dispute, that such troubles were obvious to anyone, but he did not mention the troubles in the flesh which one who does not marry may encounter. Perhaps that was too close to the bone for Paul to wish to speak of.

Last year there was a symposium of seminary women at which one woman complained that everything in the seminary program was based on the assumption that the students were men. The statement was not accurate, but even if it had been, it would seem that a woman who chooses to go to seminary would know ahead of time that the majority of the students would be men and the program would naturally emphasize this. She would be prepared to be in the minority and accept the limitations imposed by this. Common sense would tell her this. I thought of John Sanders, a blind graduate of the seminary. I have never heard John complain that the whole world operates as though everybody can see. Of course the world operates that way. Most people can see. John accepts this as a matter of course, never whines or even refers to his blindness, and makes a way for himself in spite of the (to us) impossible limitations of his life.

You will remember Betty Greene, one of the founders of the Missionary Aviation Fellowship, who has flown every kind of plane except a jet. She even ferried bombers during World War II, and you were surprised that she didn't "look like a pilot." Nobody else thought she did either, and often when she would land in some foreign airfield the authorities were nonplussed to see a woman step out of the plane. "Do you fly these planes *alone*?" she was often asked. But long ago Betty had made up her mind that if she was going to make her way in a man's world she had to be a lady. She would have to compete with men in being a pilot, but she would not compete with men in being a man. She refused to try in any way to act like a man.

It is a naive sort of feminism that insists that women prove their ability to do all the things that men do. This is a distortion and a travesty. Men have never sought to prove that they can do all the things women do. Why subject women to purely masculine criteria? Women can and ought to be judged by the criteria of femininity, for it is in their femininity that they participate in the human race. And femininity has its limitations. So has masculinity. That is what we've been talking about. To do this is not to do that. To be this is not to be that. To be a woman is not to be a man. To be married is not to be single—which may mean not to have a career. To marry this man is not to marry all the others. A choice is a limitation.

# TWENTY-TWO

# Commitment, Gratitude, Dependence

Karl Barth, in his superb treatise on Man and Woman in *Church Dogmatics*, defines marriage as "the form of encounter of male and female in which the free, mutual, harmonious choice of love on the part of a particular man and woman leads to a responsibly undertaken life-union which is lasting, complete, and exclusive. It is the *telos*, the goal and center of the relationship between man and woman. The sphere of male and female is wider than that of marriage, embracing the whole complex of relations at the center of which marriage is possible."

What a difference from the casual liaisons entered into by young couples who, in seeking to be "free" have dispensed with that responsibly undertaken life-union. Their union is not responsible to anyone, it is not lasting, complete, or exclusive, and as such cannot possibly bring them the joy they so desperately hope for. All manner of alternatives have been tried and none has produced what it promised. No marriage "experiment" has any validity, lacking the essential ingredient of total and irrevocable commitment.

But how can they know commitment to one another when they have made no higher commitment? Thank God for a loyalty not only to each other but a common higher loyalty which you and Walt share— loyalty to God, whose call you've heard. That is a sound basis for marriage.

But don't be deceived. Many couples have shared this loyalty (some I know shared almost nothing else) and have found that their marriage was far from ideal. As long as we are "in the flesh" we'll have trouble in the flesh. But God knows the purpose of heart. He sees the direction a couple has taken when they have made up their minds to seek "things which are above." There is a whole world of difference between those who look only for their own happiness in this world and those who know that their true happiness lies in the will of God.

When they encounter trouble they know where to turn, for they know that they are still under the command of God, they are not forsaken. They *know* that they are insufficient in themselves, that human love breaks down, and that there is never a point at which they can say, "We've arrived," and are no longer in need of grace.

You know, I am sure, that your love is a gift. And if it is a gift you are grateful to the Giver. To acknowledge your gratitude to Him is also to acknowledge your dependence on Him, to acknowledge above all the authority of Christ. That is a good place to begin a marriage.

# TWENTY-THREE

# *You Marry a Sinner*

In the past several years I have talked to college and seminary women on marriage. What I have said to them I say to you, and it can be summed up under three headings which are three questions:

1) Who is it you marry?
2) What is marriage?
3) What makes marriage work?

First of all, who is it you marry? You marry a sinner. There's nobody else to marry. That ought to be obvious enough but when you love a man as you love yours it's easy to forget. You forget it for a while and then when something happens that ought to remind you you find yourself wondering what's the matter, how could this happen, where did things go wrong? They went wrong back in the Garden of Eden. Settle it once for all, your husband is a son of Adam. Acceptance of him—of all of him—includes acceptance of his being a sinner. He is a fallen creature, in need of the same kind of redemption all the rest of us are in need of, and liable to all the temptations which are "common to man." Our old friend Dorothy has taught me many things out of her long life of trust in God and keen observation of humanity, and one day as we were discussing friendship and marriage she said, "Well, dear, we're none of us prize packages. Just look for the essentials and skip the rest!" The prize package we think we've found is likely to contain some surprises, not all of them welcome. What a lot of heartbreak would be avoided if we could concentrate on the essentials and skip the rest. How much more we could relax with one another and enjoy all there is to enjoy.

In the service of Morning Prayer we repeat on our knees this confession: "We have erred and strayed from Thy ways like lost sheep, we have followed too much the devices and desires of our own hearts, we have offended against Thy holy laws. We have left undone those things which we ought to have done, and we have done those things which we ought not to have done, and there is no health in us."

As I say those words I sometimes think of the people who are saying them with me and I think, "I belong to this company. Lost sheep. No health in any of us."

It might not be a bad thing, even if you and Walt are Presbyterians, to say this prayer together once in a while, remembering that "we" means both of you. You will be less likely to turn into a nagging wife if you recall continually that it is not only your husband who leaves undone those things which (you think) he ought to do, and does things which (you think) he ought not to do, but that you, too, have erred and strayed like a lost sheep, sinning daily by omission and commission.

The consciousness that we are alike in our need of redemption is a liberating one. For there will be times when you find yourself accusing, criticizing, resenting. You begin, almost without realizing that you are doing it, to make a mental list of offenses, anticipating the day when some straw will break the camel's back and you can recite the whole list, sure to add at the end "and another thing . . . !" But you will find yourself disarmed utterly, and your accusing spirit transformed into loving forgiveness the moment you remember that you did, in fact, marry only a sinner, and *so did he*. It's grace you both need.

> 'Tis grace hath brought us safe thus far
> And grace will lead us home.

One of the silliest statements ever to catch the public imagination came out of that silly movie *Love Story*—"Love is never having to say you're sorry." If it doesn't make you sorry to hurt somebody you love, what in the world would ever make you sorry? You *do* need forgiveness. You *do* need to forgive. And it is a wonderfully healing thing to confess your sin to the one you've sinned against and to ask for his forgiveness. At times when you are thinking to yourself that it's high time he asked for yours, remember that you are equal in your need of redemption. There's no keeping of score in love.

Nor is love blind. In fact, the one who truly loves sees clearly the truth about the beloved which is hidden from other eyes. It is perhaps because the beloved makes the very sunshine brighter and the whole world sing that it is not always easy to remember that he is a sinner. But when love becomes an everyday fact that we live with we begin to discover imperfections to which we respond either lovingly or unlovingly.

Sara Teasdale has expressed the loving response in "Appraisal":

> Never think she loves him wholly,
> Never believe her love is blind,
> All his faults are locked securely
> In a closet of her mind;
> All his indecisions folded
> Like old flags that time has faded,
> Limp and streaked with rain,
> And his cautiousness like garments
> Frayed and thin, with many a stain—
> Let them be, oh let them be.
> There is treasure to outweigh them,
> His proud will that sharply stirred,
> Climbs as surely as the tide.
> Senses strained too taut to sleep,
> Gentleness to beast and bird,
> Humor flickering hushed and wide,
> As the moon on moving water,
> And a tenderness too deep
> To be gathered in a word.

So—you marry a sinner. And you love, accept, and forgive that sinner as you yourself expect to be loved, accepted, and forgiven. You know that "all have sinned and come short of the glory of God," and this includes your husband who comes short, also, of some of the glories you expected to find in him. Come to terms with this once and for all and then walk beside him as "heirs together of the grace of life."

# TWENTY-FOUR

# *You Marry a Man*

You marry not only a sinner but a man. You marry a man, not a woman. Strange how easy it seems to be for some women to expect their husbands to be women, to act like women, to do what is expected of women. Instead of that they are men, they act like men, they do what is expected of men and thus they do the unexpected. They surprise their wives by being men and some wives wake up to the awful truth that it was not, in fact, a *man* that they wanted after all. It was marriage, or some vague idea of marriage, which provided the fringe benefits they were looking for—a home, children, security, social status. But somehow marriage has also insinuated into their cozy lives this unpredictable, unmanageable, unruly creature called a man. He is likely to be bigger and louder and tougher and hungrier and dirtier than a woman expects, and she finds that bigger feet make bigger footprints on the newly washed kitchen floor; they make a bigger noise on the stairs. She learns that what makes her cry may make him laugh. He eats far more than seems necessary or even reasonable to a woman who never ceases her vigil against excess weight. When he takes a shower his broader dimensions mean more water used and a greater surface for water to cling to and therefore she finds that the towels get much wetter and he probably doesn't hang them up folded in three as she wants him to in order to display the monogram. He may not hang them up at all. He won't use a washcloth which means he consumes three times as much soap as she does. When she cleans the bathroom she finds she has to clean in places she never had to clean before. He's a toothpaste-tube twister instead of a roller. Anything he does which seems to her inexplicable or indefensible she dismisses with "Just like a man!" as though this were a condemnation or at best an excuse instead of a very good reason for thanking God. It is a man she married, after all, and she is lucky if he acts like a man.

"Men are men," Gertrude Behanna says, "they are not women. Women are women. They are not men." It's another of those simple facts which are not always so simple to remember.

I know it's hard for you to imagine this early in the game, but some day you may think to yourself (you might even say it out loud), "I'm not sure my husband understands me." You are probably right. He doesn't. He's a man. You're a woman. There are some areas in which ne'er the twain shall meet and we should be glad of that. Although there are times when we are frustrated and infuriated by the inability to fathom the depths of another personality, who can deny the fascination of mystery, of knowing that there are depths we haven't plumbed?

There is a story in the Bible which tells of a man who was able to answer all a woman's questions. The Queen of Sheba went to Jerusalem to test Solomon, the famous king, with hard questions. She went with pomp and splendor—appropriate to so momentous an encounter. We have heard of the wisdom and justice of Solomon, but no mention is made of his longsuffering. This story reveals it, for it is said that the queen "told him all that was on her mind." That must have taken a long time. Not many men would want to hear all that was on a woman's mind, but apparently the king listened, for "Solomon answered all her questions, there was nothing hidden from Solomon which he could not explain to her." What a man he must have been to have command of all the answers and the patience to make all the explanations necessary to satisfy a powerful female potentate who had doubtless come with skepticism and perhaps jealousy and scorn. But she was thoroughly convinced. He won her over, and she saw his wisdom. She surveyed also the house that he had built, the food of his table, the seating of his officials, the attendance of his servants and their clothing, and his burnt offerings which he offered at the house of the Lord. When she had seen it all, "there was no more spirit in her." The display took all the wind out of the queen's sails. She did manage to pull herself together sufficiently to commend him and remind him of God's blessing on him. When she had presented him with the gifts she had brought and received gifts from him, there was nothing left for her to do but go home.

Not many men can do what Solomon did. Not many men ought to try. And a woman who sets out to test a man with hard questions should be forewarned that she may end up with no more spirit in her, nothing to do but turn around and go back where she came from. It is probably not only a safer course but much wiser not to tell a man everything that is on your mind, not to press him with hard questions. Leave room for mystery.

When we were preparing for a panel on marriage for college women, five panelists gathered in our house to discuss which topic each of us was to cover. In the course of what became a highly animated conversation I suggested that somebody ought to talk about crying. This surprised some of them. What on earth did I mean? Well, women cry. Many of them don't do it often, of course, but it's a possibility a man should be ready for. Nothing is more baffling to a young husband than his wife's tears—usually at most unexpected moments and for seemingly wholly unexplainable reasons. His anxious questions get nowhere, and her attempts to explain only increase his anxiety. Men ought to be warned that this is likely to occur, and women ought to be warned that it's no use trying to explain. It's just one of the things that prove that men are men and women are women.

This argument was met with loud protest. "Why, I'm sure I don't cry more than once a week!" one woman insisted. Your stepfather happened to pass through the living room just at this juncture. He had been perplexed that we were to have a panel at all. What was there to talk about? A panel on marriage? With five people as panelists? For an hour? What would we say? When he overheard this sample he left quickly.

Later he and I were visiting in the home of an exceedingly attractive couple in their thirties. He was an athlete, she had been a beauty queen and a model.

"Tell them about your panel on marriage," Add said to me.

"Panel on marriage?" said the husband, looking blank.

I told him what it was and where we did it.

"But—what is there to say?" he asked. His wife and I looked at each other. For some reason women have no difficulty imagining a discussion on marriage. Men find it unimaginable. But when I told them about the preliminary discussion on crying, it was the husband who understood at once.

"I know exactly what you mean!" he said. "Sometimes I come home from the office feeling great. I go to bed at night pleased with myself, and I lie there with my hands locked under my head on the pillow, thinking about that brilliant decision I made at work and that beautiful hook-shot I made down at the gym. Then all of a sudden I hear a snuffle.

" 'Are you crying?' I say.

"(snuffle) 'No.'

" 'Come on now. You're crying!'

" 'No I'm not!' (snuffle, snuffle)

" 'What's wrong?' I say.

" 'Nothing!' she says, and she's still snuffling. Well, I've been married long enough to know that this is going to be a three-hour deal, and it's going to mean lights, robes, and coffee!"

The whole time he was telling this, his wife was sitting on the edge of her chair, grinning from ear to ear. They both knew exactly what I was talking about. They agreed that it deserved some mention on the panel.

But I can't leave this part of the discussion without adding that men cry too. I am not drawing simple dichotomies here, as though all women and no men cry. I know men who weep much more readily than I do. Know your man. Know that there are things that make him different from you. His masculinity will help to explain some of them.

# TWENTY-FIVE

# You Marry
# a Husband

The third thing to remember is that you marry a husband. For you, Val, I doubt that this will be as difficult to remember as it is for women who have had brothers and sisters, and who have known their own fathers. For some of them it is easy to transfer what they expected of fathers, brothers, sisters, mothers or girlfriends to their unfortunate husbands and this is a burden no man can bear. He stands in a relationship to you which is totally new and unique and it is going to require a measure of maturity for both of you to enter into it.

If you succumb to the temptation to expect your husband to fulfill all the roles of all the relationships you have had prior to marriage you will learn that this is asking too much. He needs his male friends, you need your female ones, even though your marriage and your home take top priority in your interest. Try not to put your poor husband in the indefinable position of having to listen to all your troubles, little or big (and your classification of them will most likely differ from his), to discuss hairdos and recipes and diets and menus and the color of the living room draperies as well as topics that may interest both of you far more. Now I know men who take a lively interest in their wives' hairdos and recipes, men who actually go shopping for their wives' clothes, and I even know of one husband who makes his wife's clothes. Some men want to know what you're planning for dinner and want to rearrange furniture. If he's interested, that changes the whole picture. If he's not, talk it over with somebody who is if you want to talk it over at all.

I know I'm sticking my neck out to mention food and clothes and furniture at all. The stereotypical "traditional" wife is interested in nothing else. That's nonsense, of course. We could as easily accuse men of talking only about cars, sports, or the stock market. Anyone, man or woman, who has a live and curious mind may be interested in food, furniture, sports, and the stock market for after all, all of us eat, we need furniture, recreation, and money. Why shouldn't we talk about them occasionally? But it doesn't mean that nothing else is of interest. I like to cook, and good cooking takes a lot of time, talent, and imagination. I talk about it sometimes. But when I'm peeling an onion I'm not thinking about onions. My mind ranges far from the sink. A man has to drive a car, he probably likes to drive a car, and he wants a good one. He talks about cars sometimes. But when he's driving it his mind may be on theology or big-game hunting or even on his family.

All I'm suggesting is that you not be a bore. Some topics will interest your mother more than they will interest your husband. Remember he's a husband!

Your father used to say that every woman needed three husbands: one to bring home the bacon, one to love her, and one to fix things around the house. It is a lot to expect of one man, and a woman ought not to judge her husband solely on the basis of how good he is with a hammer. If a woman happens to have had a father who fixed faucets and doorknobs and loose tiles, who went around oiling hinges and planing sticking drawers without even being asked, she expects her husband to do the same. What kind of man is it, she asks, who is no good with wrenches and screwdrivers?

There are women who have grown up in athletic families where all the boys played football or base-ball, and the whole family slept, ate, and drank sports all year round. It comes as a shock to such women if they marry men who have no use for team sports but would rather fish or hike. A young wife I know was dumbfounded at the array of gear required to keep her husband "in shape." He had two or three sports going at once and on some days had to change clothes two or three times in order to meet the requirements. She found herself going around picking up "all these *outfits*!" as she said, and having to keep up with the laundry. She just wasn't prepared for that when she acquired a husband.

I believe a woman, in order to be a good wife, must be (among other things) both sensual and maternal. Marriage entails sensuality—an appreciation of the body and the senses as distinguished from the intellect—but a woman must also have a certain maternal feeling toward her husband. Not that she babies him. Deep resentment is expressed sometimes by women who feel that their husbands want to be babied. But a wife must want to take care of her husband and to minister to him *as gladly* as a mother ministers to her child.

The husband has a corresponding task. The word husband carries the connotation of conserving, caring for, managing, or protecting. A wife needs to allow herself to be cherished. Let him "husband" you. This is easy for certain women. It is perhaps too easy, and they may not only allow themselves to be cherished but they require coddling. You know me well enough to know that this is not what I mean. You have not been coddled. Growing up with Indians taught you to accept very matter-of-factly what most of us "civilized" people would call hardship. You knew from the beginning that you were not expected to fuss, and you learned your lesson well. You have been independent, ever since the days when you would go off with the Indians for a whole day's fishing or gathering, leaving me behind. On your first day of school in the States the school bus went right past you and I had to drive you down to the school. The children had all gone in when we arrived, but you marched with courage into that completely new place, carrying your lunch box and holding your head up.

So I am not fearful of your being a clinging vine. But do let him cherish you. He is your husband.

# TWENTY-SIX

# *You Marry a Person*

Fourth, you must remember that you marry a person. I put this fourth on the list, not first. I have come to treat the word "person" rather gingerly in recent years because it is so overused. I hear people talk of wanting to be treated "not as a woman but as a human being," or "as a person." I hear words like "chairperson" and "spokesperson," and even absurdities such as the "freshperson class" and "personhole covers." There is something seriously distorted about this view of humanity. I don't want anybody treating me as a "person" *rather* than as a woman. Our sexual differences are the terms of our life, and to obscure them in any way is to weaken the very fabric of life itself. When they are lost, we are lost. Some women fondly imagine a new beginning of liberty, but it is in reality a new bondage, more bitter than anything they seek to be liberated from.

I want to know not "people" but men and women. I am interested in men as men, in women as women, and when you marry you marry a man because he is a man, and being a man he becomes your husband. This is the glory of marriage—two separate and distinct kinds of beings are unified.

But when you have accepted him as a sinner, as a man, and as a husband, you must still remember that he is a person. As a person, he has a name. Nothing more infallibly reveals your attitude to another person than the name you call him by.

There are those who never call each other anything. I have heard a husband shout out a question or a comment to his wife from another room without using any form of address at all. I have heard wives do the same, and I have heard both refer to their spouses only by the third person pronoun. It seems to me that those who do this have never recognized or have forgotten the person they married. He has become a fixture.

Then there are those who call each other "mommy" and "daddy." This is fine when speaking of the other to the children. But for a man to call his wife "mommy" is a dead giveaway. The magic has gone out of that marriage. Is he her lover still, or has he become her little boy? Is this a relationship that is still growing toward maturity, or is it regressing?

I would be the last to complain of endearing names. I like them. It does my heart good to hear a man call a woman "darling" or even "cream puff" if he wants to. It shows she's special to him. Katherine Mansfield, whose tender and delightful love letters have all been published, unabridged, called her husband "Bogey" and he called her "Wig." All I ask is that a couple call each other *something*. That they show by the way they address each other, in public or in bed, that they recognize a personality.

One of the most joyful discoveries of life is that in recognizing, affirming, and comforting another person we find ourselves recognized, affirmed, and comforted. It is a dead-end street to set out to know yourself or to "find" yourself or to define "who am I?"

"It is plain that no man can arrive at the true knowledge of himself without first having contemplated the divine character," wrote John Calvin in the Introduction to his great *Institutes*. And it is in relation to other people that we ourselves become full persons. "No man is an island." We are called to fellowship with God and we are called to fellowship with each other. Marriage is the most intimate and continuous relationship into which two people may enter, and as such provides the most uninterrupted opportunity for fulfillment of the personality. This is not to say, of course, that only married people can know fulfillment. The measure of self-giving is the measure of fulfillment. There are married people who have not learned the first lesson in self-giving. There are single people who have gone very far along the road. It has always seemed to me relatively easy to give myself for my husband first because I loved him with all my heart, and then because the rewards were usually more obvious and more immediate than they may be in other relationships. Loving a wife, as the Bible says (and surely it applies to loving a husband as well), is the same as loving your own body.

But if your husband is a person this means that you must accept the mystery of his personhood. We have already spoken of how men and women do not and cannot perfectly understand one another. And this is not simply because of sexual barriers. Persons of the same sex find also a closed door. Your husband is known fully only to God, and stands in a sense alone before Him. God said to Abraham, "Walk before Me and be thou perfect." He did not suggest that Abraham could walk before Sarah and be perfect. Ultimately he is God's man. He is free, and you must always reverence this freedom. There are questions you have no right to ask, matters into which you must not probe, and secrets you must be content never to know.

"Hasn't a wife a right to know all?"

No. She cannot take or even ask for what is not given, and there are things a man cannot and ought not to give. The deeps call only to God.

# TWENTY-SEVEN

# *Forsaking All Others*

Finally, you marry this sinner, this man, this husband, and this person. Marriage is a choice of one above all others. Each partner promises to forsake all others, and the Bible says that man will leave his father and mother and "cleave" to his wife. Any choice we ever make in life instantly limits us. To choose to take this man as your husband is to choose not to take every other man on earth. When you decide to marry this particular sinner you have committed yourself to putting up with his particular sins even though you don't have a very clear idea of what they will be. You will begin at once to find them out, and as you do, remind yourself that you married *this* sinner. You can always look at other sinners and thank God you don't have to live with their varieties of failure, but then what kind of sins would you choose if you could choose which ones to live with? It's a good thing you are not asked. You love this man who happens to be this kind of sinner and you do your best to accept, to forgive, to overlook, to forbear, and, perhaps, in the mercy of God, to help him to overcome.

When you decide to marry this particular man you have decided not to marry every other man, and this particular man has limitations. You don't start right in on his limitations like the lady in *My Fair Lady* who'll

> redecorate your home
> from the cellar to the dome
> and then go on to the enthralling fun
> of overhauling *you*!

You don't marry him with the idea of a complete renovation. When asked for advice for women contemplating marriage Mrs. Billy Graham said, "Marry somebody to whom *you* are willing to adjust."

If you are a very generous wife, you may perhaps allow that your husband lives up to 80 percent of your expectations. The other 20 percent you may want to change. You may, if you choose, pick away at that 20 percent for the rest of your married life and you probably will not reduce it by very much. Or you may choose to skip that and simply enjoy the 80 percent that is what you hoped for.

You marry *this* person. He may be the person who was, ten years ago, the "Big Man on Campus." You were attracted to him because he was a football star or the president of the student body or the most articulate leader of campus protests. But life settles down to the humdrum. Marriage is no house party, it's not a college campus or a stimulating political row or an athletic contest, and the man's having been a spellbinding orator or a great halfback somehow does not seem terribly significant anymore. But you ought now and then to remember what he was, to ask yourself what it was, really, that caught your eye. Come now, you will say to yourself, you didn't marry him because he was a great halfback, did you? No, you married this *person*. Whatever the inner qualities were that enabled him to do the things he did then are still a part of this person that you go to bed with and eat breakfast with and wrestle over the monthly budget with. He is a person with the same potentials he had when you married him. Your responsibility now is not merely to bat your eyelashes and tell him how wonderful he is (but breathes there a man with soul so dead as not to be cheered by a little of that?) but to *appreciate*, genuinely and deeply, what he is, to support and encourage and draw out of him those qualities that you originally saw and admired.

I had been a widow for thirteen years when the man who was to become your stepfather proposed. It seemed to me the miracle that could never happen. That any man had wanted me the first time was astonishing. I had gone through high school and college with very few dates. But to be wanted again was almost beyond imagination. I told this man that I knew there were women waiting for him who could offer him many things I couldn't offer—things like beauty and money. But, I said, "There's one thing I can give you that no woman on earth can outdo me in and that's appreciation." The perspective of widowhood had taught me that.

Some years ago there was a series of letters to

columnist Ann Landers on the subject of men who snore. Wives wrote in complaining of the countless hours of lost sleep and the irritation of that awful noise beside them in the bed. Others wrote offering solutions, but the discussion came to an end with one letter, "Snoring is the sweetest music in the world. Ask any widow."

How often I have sat in a roomful of people and heard a wife contradict, criticize, belittle, or sneer at her husband before the rest of the company and I have with difficulty restrained myself from leaping from my chair, going over and shaking that woman by the shoulders and saying, "Do you realize what you've got?" She doesn't. She hasn't my perspective, of course. If only there were some way for every wife to have the experience of losing her husband for a little time—even of thinking that he's dead—in order to regain the perspective she needs for genuine appreciation.

Your growth toward maturity will bring you a wider perspective. The Apostle Paul, always desirous that his converts should move on into spiritual maturity, prayed for the Colossian Christians that they might see things from God's point of view by being given spiritual insight and understanding. What could be a greater help to a wife than to see her husband as God sees him? God has created him, formed him, redeemed him, he is His. God is bringing him to perfection and is not by any means through with him yet. We are all unfinished, a long way from what we ought to be, but if we can look at ourselves and one another from God's point of view we'll know where we ought to be going and in which direction our relationship should move.

Not long after my second marriage we were invited to speak as a team in a church whose pastor had himself been recently remarried. He and his first wife, who had died of cancer, had been in college with me. I wanted to know what he had learned in a year of second marriage. Without hesitation he told me.

"I've learned that Marcie can give me things Sue could never have given. Sue gave me things Marcie can't give. So I've learned appreciation—for both of them. I appreciate Marcie for exactly what she is, in a way I hadn't the capacity to appreciate Sue."

I know that you will not be shocked by my asking the question, nor by the man's making comparisons between Wives One and Two. Why shouldn't he? It's natural, and the comparison between Marcie and Sue was made not to disparage either, but to appreciate each fully for what she was. To the Christian who has prayed for years to be led to the right partner and who believes that the one he marries is indeed God's choice for him, it is reasonable to conclude that the personality given is the one that best complements his own, the one that meets his needs in ways he could not himself have foreseen or chosen. It is the very differences themselves that open our eyes to what we are and, if we pray for the spiritual insight and understanding that Paul prayed for, we see them as God sees them and appreciate the glorious imagination of the Creator who made them.

# TWENTY-EIGHT

# Dynamic, Not Static

We've talked about who it is you're marrying. Now what is marriage? You've had Barth's definition. I can't improve on that, but there are four things which, as you live out the days and weeks and years with your husband, marriage turns out to be.

It is a dynamic, not a static, relationship. It gets either better or worse. As people either grow or deteriorate, relationships between them must grow or deteriorate. A common explanation offered for marital incompatibility is "We outgrew each other." A couple meets in high school or college, shares youthful interests, marries, begins to find out that "making it" in the world may not be as much of a lark as making friends, making grades, or making touchdowns was, back on campus. Responsibility begins to close in and bills have to be paid, decisions made, hard work done for which there are no public (and all too often no private) rewards. It's been said that if a couple doesn't grow together they grow apart. But for the couple who have in all seriousness said their vows before God and in the presence of witnesses the possibility of growing apart need not be allowed. It need never be something which "happens to" them, as though they were bystanders injured by some force which they were powerless to protect themselves from. They have willed to love and live together. They stand, not helpless, but in relation to God, each responsible to fulfill his vows to the other. Each determines to do the will of God so that together they move toward "the measure of the stature of the fullness of Christ." And, if God is viewed as the apex of a triangle of which they are the two base points, movement toward Him necessarily decreases the distance between them. Drawing near to God means drawing nearer to each other, and this means growth and change. They are being changed into the same image from glory to glory. There is no such thing as stagnation, or that relatively innocent-sounding word incompatibility.

There are tensions. The strength of a great cathedral lies in the thrust and counterthrust of its buttresses and arches. Each has its own function and each its peculiar strength. This is the way I see the dynamics of a good marriage. It is not strength pitted against weakness. It is two kinds of strength, each meant to fortify the other in special ways. We have already talked about the sailboat analogy with reference to the meaning of discipline. It is not a weakness for the boat to submit itself to the rules of sailing. That submission *is* her strength. It is the rules that enable the boat to utilize her full strength, to harness the wind and thus take to herself the wind's strength. It was not weakness in the Son of God that made Him obey the will of the Father. It was power—the power of His own will to will the Father's will.

There is in a good marriage both dependence and independence on both sides. Your husband needs you to be different from him, to be what you are alone, to be what he can never be and what he needs and wants. Only in this way can you be what you are in relation to him. Only in this way can you complement him. He depends on you to be his complement, you depend on him to be yours. He is independent of you in his differences—you are woman, distinct, wholly other, opposite. "Nevertheless," said the Apostle Paul, "in the Lord woman is not independent of man nor man of woman; for as woman was made from man so man is now born of woman. And all things are from God." Men and women cannot and must not try to live life without reference to the opposite sex. They are interdependent and are meant to acknowledge and confront one another. It is this confrontation—most clearly realized in marriage—that makes it of enormous importance that the sexes not be confused, ignored, played down or played off against each other. We need each other. A husband and wife need to be husband and wife, not buddies. The dynamics must be maintained as the Architect intended.

You have already had some experience of this process of change. You met Walt first because he was Ed's friend. When you saw him next, when you came home from college for the holidays, he interested you and you began to think of him no longer as the friend of a friend, but as your friend. Remember the evening when you were casually going about your business, cleaning up the kitchen, doing your ironing, and he stayed and stayed? You saw that he was making excuses to stay, and the realization that you interested him caused another change. He was not merely a friend anymore. Two months later you had a valentine from him, and soon after that a birthday card. At Easter you saw him again and began to wonder if you loved him. You got one or two letters during the summer, and in the fall you knew without any doubt that he loved you. Then, last Christmas, he was your fiancé, and will soon be your husband.

Friend, lover, husband. In your life together he will be many things to you. Confidant, companion, provider, strength, playmate, listener, teacher, pupil, leader, comforter, and, as Sarah saw Abraham, "lord." Each role has its glories and its limitations, each requires a different kind of response from you and this takes resilience, adaptability, maturity. Life is made exciting and interest is sustained by these dynamics so long as all are undergirded by love.

Your provider may someday lose his job. Your strength may show unexpected weakness. Your knight in armor may experience a public defeat. Your teacher may make a serious mistake that you tried to warn him about. Your lover may become a helpless patient, sick, sore, and sad, needing your presence and care every minute of the day and night. "This isn't the man I married," you will say, and it will be true. But you married him for better or for worse, in sickness and in health, and those tremendous promises took into account the possibility of radical change. That was why promises were necessary.

There are things in life which can make what seems to be a mockery out of the solemn promises. "To love, honor, and obey" your husband can seem the last ironies in the face of the unspeakable humiliations and indignities of illness. Love, honor, and obey this beaten, anguished, angry man who will not take his pill? The vows are serious. Staggeringly serious. But you did not take them trusting in your own strength to perform. The grace that enabled you to take those vows will be there to draw on when the performance of them seems impossible.

# TWENTY-NINE

# A Union

Marriage is a union. It takes two to make a union. One cannot do it. When God created man, He saw that it was not good for him to be alone, and He created a woman from and for him, specifically designed to help him, to be suitable for him, to be his mate. The woman is totally other, totally different, totally God's gift to man, and each stands in relation to the other, responsible to the other in obedience to the command of God, responsible to be a man or a woman, and, in marriage, to unite as one flesh. It is for this reason that a man leaves his parents. He forsakes all other ties in the flesh in order to establish this most intimate one of all, the only one which is a perfect union of one flesh.

There is no competition in a union. There is no playing off of one against the other, no keeping score, no making of comparisons or insistence on a fifty-fifty division of anything. Each is for the other, pulling with and not against him.

But we are human. You, being my daughter, know very well that I am human and full of flaws and make no claim that things always work flawlessly.

Once, before your father and I were married, I learned that he felt we were competing and this was a hard thing for him to take. We were both studying Spanish under an Ecuadorian lady, and she had to correct his pronunciation more often than she had to correct mine. He was not upset because he thought she was being partial. He was upset because he thought she was right. I knew nothing about it until once when we were walking together and he spoke of it. It was not that he was asking me to slow down, to "act dumb," to be an inferior student. Nothing was further from his mind. He only wanted to confess his difficulty with this competition. I recognized that I had been enjoying it, and had probably studied harder than I would have if I had not had it. He recognized that differences of gifts is one of the facts of life and he was able eventually to accept this. It was a question of feelings, not reason, and he saw it as such. Both of us began to learn—and this is a lesson which we never stop learning—that whatever gifts either of us had were not that we might flaunt them but that we might use them for the sake of other people. After we were married we discovered how our various gifts fit together astonishingly well, and thus we began to learn the lesson of 1 Corinthians 12:17, 18, "If the whole body were an eye, where would be the hearing? If the whole body were an ear, where would be the sense of smell? But as it is God arranged the organs in the body, each one of them, as he chose."

There is union in the physical body—all the members joined together in harmony and for the good of the whole, all subject to the head. So there is union in marriage, two separate persons made one in the flesh, and, if they are Christians, one in Christ, subject to His headship. If they are one in Christ, they have not only union but communion, and this is a priceless thing.

# THIRTY

# A Mirror

Marriage turns out to be a mirror. Each reflects the other, which is bound to be in some degree painful, for none of us can bear too much reality at once. A budgie in Australia named Tweetie Pie saw himself in a mirror hung near his cage, and had to be given tranquilizers because the revelation made him screech at night, fight imaginary enemies, and curl up in a corner of the cage.

Marriage is for most people the first experience in adulthood of common life—of the daily, ordinary, humble doing of duties in close contact with and mutual dependence on another person. Few have had to take responsibility on a day-to-day basis until they marry. A college roommate may have provided a little practice, but precious little housekeeping and probably no cooking or money-managing were included. These are hard realities and if marriage is the first chance you have to face up to them you may make the mistake of blaming on marriage itself, or on your spouse, difficulties which are simply a part of adult life. Life has a lot of humdrum in it. You've

110

never faced much of it alone, and when you start facing it together it's no wonder that weakness and sinfulness will be disclosed. No wonder there are surprises. You'll be catching glimpses of yourself in a mirror.

You have had some practice in the routines of living. You have planned, shopped for, and cooked meals in the past couple of years and you have done it well. But it is another matter to plan, purchase, and cook twenty-one meals a week, for fifty-two weeks. You have earned and managed your own spending money for several years, but to have to budget and carefully spend the money somebody else has earned, and make it last for two of you for a month and then for twelve months is quite a different thing.

And in such earthly matters you will be tested. You will see yourself in this context as you have not seen yourself before. You will see yourself through your husband's eyes and that will be a revelation. Sometimes you will see faults in him. It is quite likely that you are seeing in him faults you need to work on in yourself.

If you are depressed, you may notice that he is depressed. If you make it a point to be cheerful, it may surprise you what a difference it makes in your husband when he has good reason not to be cheerful. You can create a climate for him according to your attitude, and this is part of your job as a wife. The home you make and the atmosphere of that home is the world he comes back to from the world of his work. Let it be a place of beauty and peace.

# THIRTY-ONE

# A Vocation

Finally, and I think most importantly, marriage is a vocation. It is a task to which you are called. If it is a task, it means you work at it. It is not something which happens. You hear the call, you answer, you accept the task, you enter into it willingly and eagerly, you commit yourself to its disciplines and responsibilities and limitations and privileges and joys. You concentrate on it, giving yourself to it day after day in a lifelong Yes. Having said Yes to the man who asked you to marry him, you go on saying Yes to marriage.

This is easier for a woman to do, I think. Speaking from my own experience, even a woman who has a career when she marries finds it easy to make marriage her primary task, to lay down the career "with hallelujah" as Ruth Benedict said, in order to let her husband have first place. Perhaps, in the plan of God, she does not actually lay down this career. She must continue to do the work to which she was first called. I was a missionary before your father asked me to marry him, and when I married him I was still a missionary, not just a missionary's wife. The second time I married I had entered another field of work, writing, and I was not released from that job in order to become a wife, although in both cases it was clear to me that my primary vocation was marriage. If I had not been willing and eager to enter this vocation with its disciplines, responsibilities, limitations, and privileges then I ought not to have married. That seemed self-evident to me. There may be a few exceptional women who successfully combine career and marriage, but to give full attention to both at the same time is an impossibility. If a woman wants her career to have priority she will do better to stay single, for the simple scriptural reason that she was made to adapt to a man (made "for him") if she has a man.

Perhaps I am making it sound too easy. There was for me before I married the first time a long period of thought and prayer as to whether in fact the missionary calling might not actually preclude the possibility, in my case, of marriage. For some it certainly does. For Amy Carmichael it apparently did. She knew that the call of God to missionary work conflicted with her own desires to marry, and she chose not her way but His. I wondered if I was being asked to make the same kind of choice. You know my temperament, so easily convinced that the will of God is whatever I don't want to do.

But at last, in unpredictable but to us unmistakable ways (some of which I've told about elsewhere) we knew that marriage was our vocation, and as such required (what an agreeable requirement!) our commitment.

Later, however, as the demands of being a missionary or being a writer occasionally got in the way of being a good wife, I had to wrestle with the fallacious assumption that the easier or more pleasant task, that of wife, was nothing more than an evasion of responsibility. "But it is also my responsibility to be a wife," I told myself, and immediately answered back, "But you've got to go down there and teach those Indian women to read," or "When are you going to get that translation of Luke checked?" When I was both a writer and a wife I was sorely tempted to do nothing but housework because I love housework and I especially love doing it in order to make a home for a husband, but there were times when I had to tear myself away from the kitchen and get down to the study to do the harder job first, to "eat my spinach before I could have my dessert."

This is a conflict that any married man who takes his marriage and his work seriously is going to face. I said that I think it is easier for a woman to accept her marriage as a vocation because the burden of financial responsibility rests on her husband. Even in cases where a wife's income is necessary, which it was not in my case, the husband is the provider. Scripturally, he is responsible for his family. A woman I know says to her husband, "I am your wife, but you are my life." A woman is never a man's life in the same sense that a man is a woman's life, and this is the way it was meant to be—"Woman was made for man, not man for woman." But this is why it is not easy for a man to see marriage as a vocation.

And if he does not see it as such, he will not take seriously its implications.

You would like a simple formula, wouldn't you, for sorting out the priorities? We all would, and no one is going to give us one. God alone, who calls you to your task, will help you to know where the balance lies as you weigh your responsibilities before Him, and pray and trust. "The just shall live by faith" is the rule in marriage as in all other spheres of life, and there is no other rule that covers all the vicissitudes.

Marriage is not the sole task to which any of us is called. Women who have no career as such are certainly called to a variety of tasks besides marriage. Parenthood is a task and one which, like a career, all too often eclipses the vocation of marriage so that a couple forgets that they have been called to each other and thinks only of the family. As a minister's wife you will have tasks in the church which demand time and attention. Every task requires faith. All must be recognized and accepted or rejected by faith, believing that the God who orders all things can order and direct your life so that it is not a selfish one lived "in flowery beds of ease," nor one so cluttered and hectic that the peace of God cannot rule.

And the word selfish brings us to the principle of sacrifice. Let's settle it forever—if a Christian life requires sacrifice, a Christian marriage requires sacrifice, the laying down of your life for the other, which is the central principle of Christianity. But laying down your life every day for your husband is to me not the most difficult kind of sacrifice. It doesn't usually feel anything like sacrifice. It doesn't often hurt. But when the two of you must together sacrifice yourselves for others it can feel more like it. After all I've said about your responsibility to each other, about the seriousness of this vocation of marriage, about the necessity of taking up your task, I still must remind you that the principle of the cross enters into the heart of marriage. Paul wrote to the Corinthians that because "the time is short" those who had wives should live as though they had none. Plenty of married men manage to live this way—with a blithe and thoughtless disregard for their wives and families. This is not what Paul had in mind. He was writing about the need to live life under God. He speaks of the inevitable tensions—"the unmarried woman or girl is anxious about the affairs of the Lord, how to be holy in body and spirit; but the married woman is anxious about wordly affairs, how to please her husband." Paul does not favor anxiety—"Have no anxiety about anything," he told the Philippians. But his reason for mentioning these things is "to promote good order and to secure your undivided devotion to the Lord." That devotion may at times require the laying down of your lives together for the sake of others. At other times your devotion to your husband will be accepted as devotion to the Lord. "Inasmuch as ye have done it unto one of the least of these my brethren, ye have done it unto me"—Jesus' words are proof that the way we treat other people (including, don't ever forget, your

116

husband) is the way we treat Him and is accepted as that.

So marriage is a vocation. You are called to it. Accept marriage, then, as a God-given task. Throw yourself into it with joy. Do it heartily, with faith, prayer, and thanksgiving.

# What Makes
## a Marriage Work

Before I recommend the four things which I believe
make a marriage work I have to acknowledge that
there have been countless apparently very workable
marriages in which these things mattered very little
or not at all.

I think of Eugenia and Guayaquil. Eugenia, a
Quichua Indian girl in her mid-teens, came to work
as our housegirl in Shandia. To our surprise, she
brought along a boy of about eleven whom she
introduced as her husband. They moved in, not
exactly bag and baggage, for I think it was just
bag—an Indian carrying net, to be precise. Eugenia
did the housework, Guayaquil went to school. He
was hoping to make it through the sixth grade,
which was as far as the mission school took boys in
those days. When he came home from school he did
whatever Eugenia told him to do—chopped wood or
built a fire in the stove or hauled water, and sometimes chopped onions or stirred things or washed
dishes, and it was a very convenient arrangement
for all of us.

Eugenia's older brother Gervacio was married to

Guayaquil's younger sister Carmela, a sweet little girl with huge dark eyes and a shy giggle. The mother of Guayaquil and Carmela had died when they were small and the father had decided that the easiest way to see that they were properly taken care of was to give them to their respective promised spouses. So they were given at an earlier age than would have been customary, but both marriages seemed completely successful. I asked one of the Indian women if these couples actually slept together. She whooped with laughter and said (her colloquialism loses a lot in translation), "No wife sleeps closer to her husband than Carmela!"

We watched how well polygamy worked in the Auca tribe. Our house adjoined that of Dabu who had three wives. During the day we watched them together while their husband was out hunting. Their house, like ours, had no walls. Never once did we hear an argument, or see the slightest sign of friction between those women. Dabu was faithful to them so far as anyone knew (and everyone knew practically everything about everybody) and very generous in having taken them on, for all were widows with children of their own who would have had no one to hunt meat for them if Dabu had not been so bighearted.

We have known "mixed" marriages between people of very different culture or race which seemed to work happily.

Richard Hooker, the great English theologian, married the daughter of the landlady who kept the house where he stayed when he preached in London. She was, according to a friend, "a clownish silly woman who brought him neither beauty nor portion. The marriage was a misfortune and a mistake." That was the friend's judgment. Hooker himself was satisfied with Joan, calling her his "well-beloved wife," and writing, "Woman was even in her first estate framed by nature not only after in time but inferior in excellency also unto men, howbeit in so due and sweet proportion as being presented before our eyes might be sooner perceived than defined. And even herein doth lie the reason why that kind of love which is the perfectest ground of wedlock is seldom able to yield any reason of itself."

It is a touching statement coming from such a man. As to whether he had scriptural ground for believing that woman is "inferior in excellency" to man we shall look into later, but to him it must have seemed self-evident and hence in need of no higher authority. He must, however, have known "that kind of love which is the perfectest ground of wedlock," and no one can argue with him on that.

# Acceptance of Divine Order

One thing that makes a marriage work is the acceptance of a divine order. Either there is an order or there is not, and if there is one which is violated disorder is the result—disorder on the deepest level of the personality. I believe there is an order, established in the creation of the world, and I believe that much of the confusion that characterizes our society is the result of the violation of God's design. The blueprint has been lost. Everybody is guessing at how the building is supposed to look.

Yesterday the Apollo-Soyuz mission, the American-Russian rendezvous in space, was completed. What staggering complexities had to function and fit and work together perfectly for ten days in order to bring those capsules to union, then to separate them and set them down on their appointed targets in Russia and in the pathless Pacific at the appointed minutes. (There was a variation in the American capsule's timing of twenty-four seconds in ten days.) But there had been a design. Everything was ordered and planned. Everything went according to that plan, and what pride and relief we all felt because it did.

What a relief it is to know that there is a divine design. This knowledge is the secret of serenity. Jesus is the perfect example of a human life lived in serenity and obedience to the Father's will. He moved through the events of His life without fuss or hurry, He met men and women with grace, He was able to say, "I do always those things that please the Father"—and it must have been with no variations of even twenty-four seconds. At the end of His time with the disciples as He sat with them at supper, knowing what was about to take place, He demonstrated to them that the knowledge of His origin and destiny gave Him power to do things which to them would have been unthinkable. "Jesus, knowing that He came from God and was going to God, rose from supper and took a towel. . . ." In the face of the betrayal that He knew was coming, in the face of His own death, He took the place of a slave and washed the disciples' feet. He could do that because He knew who He was and whose He was. He could face also the events of the coming night and day. It was not weakness which enabled Him to become a slave. It was not resignation that took Him to Calvary. He had both accepted and willed the Father's will.

You and I can be steadied, directed, and held by the knowledge of where we came from and where we are going. To know that the whole world moves in harmony at God's bidding is wonderfully stabilizing.

The notion of hierarchy comes from the Bible. The words superior and inferior refer originally to position, not to intrinsic worth. A person sitting in the top of a stadium would be superior to—higher up than—a person on the front row. Cherubim and seraphim were superior to archangels, archangels to angels, and man was "made a little lower than the angels." The earth and its creatures were formed prior to man, so man's position in God's scale is not necessarily determined by the chronology of creation, for that would give the animals a superior place. His position was assigned to him when he was commanded to subdue the earth and have dominion over the fish of the sea and over the birds of the air and over every living thing that moves upon the earth. "Thou hast put all things under his feet," wrote the Psalmist.

The psalms are full of expressions of God's authority and control, of measurement, limitation, direction. Psalm 104, for example, speaks of it: "Thou didst set the earth on its foundations, so that it should never be shaken . . . The mountains rose, the valleys sank down to the place which Thou didst appoint for them. Thou didst set a bound which they should not pass . . . Thou hast made the moon to mark the seasons; the sun knows its time for setting . . . When thou sendest forth thy spirit they are created."

The Book of Job describes perfection of plan, measurement, boundary, and harmony: "Where were you when I laid the foundation of the earth? Tell me if you have understanding. Who determined its measurements—surely you know! Or who stretched the line upon it? On what were its bases sunk, or who laid its cornerstone when the morning stars sang together, and all the sons of God shouted for joy?" The same chapter uses expressions such as "shut in the sea with doors," "prescribed bounds," "commanded the morning," "caused the dawn to know its place," "gates of death," "gates of deep darkness," "the way to the dwelling of light," "the place of darkness," "storehouses of the snow," "the place where light is distributed," "a way for the thunderbolt." A place for everything and everything in its place. Job, a man overwhelmed by his own physical sufferings and material losses, is brought to a new and deep knowledge of who God is and a recognition that all is wholly under His command.

The stars have kept to their courses, the seas to their boundaries. The moon sets, the sun rises, the tides ebb and flow. Animals answer to their proper nature and green things grow and produce flower and fruit in their assigned seasons.

In startling contrast the Letter of Jude refers to angels who "failed in their high duties and abandoned their proper sphere," or, in another translation, "did not keep their own position," and, as a result had to be "deprived by God of both light and liberty."

Angels and men, so far as we know, are the only creatures who have been guilty of this refusal to keep their appointed places. "Even the stork in the heavens knows her time," wrote Jeremiah, "and the turtledove, swallow, and crane keep the time of their coming; but my people know not the ordinance of the Lord."

# THIRTY-FOUR

# Equality Is Not a Christian Ideal

If we accept the idea of hierarchy we need to know where the lines are drawn.

A dean of a small church-related college was asked to relax some of the rules a little to make them more "relevant," more "realistic," more "acceptable to today's students." But this dean had been in the business long enough to know that this request would come every year. Every year the student newspaper would carry editorials on the cut system, dormitory regulations, the grading system, and compulsory chapel. (You already know that this was some years ago—students today have hardly heard of any of those things.) You could compare copies from 1926 and 1956 and find similar complaints.

"Wherever you draw the lines," the dean told them, "is where the battle will be."

In the short ten months of your life before your father died he had to draw only one line for you that I can recall. He made it quite clear that you were not to touch his books. You had pulled one from the bottom shelf and torn a page and got a spanking from him, and from then on you understood perfectly (a baby's understanding is usually way ahead of his parents' estimate) that you were not to go near them. But I can still see that little face, quizzical, self-assertive, mischievous, and plainly defiant, as you crawled slowly toward the bookcase, peeping back over your shoulder at us, testing the line. We watched silently, also testing. You kept on. A tiny finger was raised from the floor and inched toward the books. "Valerie." Pause. The finger poised in mid-air, the look still defiant. Silence. Then the finger moved, ever so slightly. "No." The finger stopped, the expression relaxed, changed suddenly to purposefulness, and you crawled away as though you had urgent business elsewhere.

Lines must be drawn. The universe is run by laws which can be relied on. Not only do college deans and parents draw lines in order to control students and children. Any business has to be run by certain clearly defined principles. A job description is given to an applicant, and if he qualifies for the job and accepts it, he accepts also the boundaries set for him and the responsibilities that go with it.

But the great question for us women is, where have the lines been drawn? Is a woman required to be subject to her husband? May a woman be ordained to the ministry of the church? Is she subordinate to men in all areas of life? Many women readily accept the notion of created order but consider men and women to have been created "equal."

Equality is not really a Christian ideal. It is, in the first place, very hard to get at what people mean when they speak of equality. Surely they can't mean that men and women are like two halves of an hourglass or an orange. Jacques Barzun in his *House of Intellect* says, "Superior and inferior can be determined only with respect to a single quality for a single purpose . . . Men are incommensurable and must be deemed equal . . . Equality is but one of man's qualities and among the most dispensable."

Men and women are equal, we may say, in having been created by God. Both male and female are created in His image. They bear the divine stamp. They are equally called to obedience and responsibility, but there are differences in the responsibilities. Both Adam and Eve sinned and are equally guilty. Therefore both are equally the objects of God's grace.

The statement "All men are created equal" is a political one, referring to a single quality for a single purpose. C. S. Lewis called this a "legal fiction," useful, necessary, but not by any means always desirable. Marriage is one place where it doesn't belong at all. Marriage is not a political arena. It is a union of two opposites. It is a confusion to speak of "separate but equal," or "opposite but equal" in referring to this unique union of two people who have become, because they were made different in order that they might thus become, one flesh.

# THIRTY-FIVE

# *Heirs of Grace*

There is a rabbit nibbling clover just under the window where I sit at the typewriter. Two men are standing in a small motor boat that moves by in the harbor, and two mourning doves sit side by side on the telephone wire. The wild roses are in full bloom now, nearly covering the split-rail fence across the road. It is hard to stay at the typewriter on such a morning. I would like to walk with you down the beach and find a hollow in a dune where we could sit and talk.

Your airletter came this morning, written just after your arrival in Amsterdam. You wrote of small, vine-covered thatched cottages and tall, majestic stone houses, of windows with sheer lace-bordered curtains and an abundance of plants and flowers, of neat farmland with canals bordering each plot. You noticed order and cleanliness. Cape Cod has some charming towns, of which Chatham is one, also neat and orderly. Men were out cutting the weeds from curbstones yesterday. The weathered shingle cottages have white curtains. There are many neat vegetable gardens surrounded by wire fences to keep out the rabbits. (Yesterday's count when I went to the post office on the bicycle was forty-four.)

What is this joy which we feel in order and design? Isn't it the same kind of pleasure we experience in the rhythm (which is the predictability) of music, the pattern of an Oriental rug, the measured movements of a dance, the unimprovable form of any true work of art? Our joy is in the very discipline of the thing. The discipline doesn't stifle, it gives power, it makes beauty possible. Why shouldn't it be so when we consider the glorious hierarchical order too? Each being plays its part in the music, in the pattern, in the dance, and in playing it in accord with the Creator's instructions finds its fullest joy.

This is a grace, and there is no more beautiful expression in the Bible to describe a married couple than Peter's "heirs together of the grace of life." The context of this phrase is interesting. Peter is writing to exiles about how they ought to conduct themselves in the countries to which they have been scattered. Their obedience to authority may ultimately lead the surrounding peoples to glorify God. Servants are to submit to their masters, whether they are good or bad, for Christ suffered unjustly and it is His example they are exhorted to follow. Married women are to adapt themselves to their husbands, following the example of Sarah who obeyed Abraham. Husbands are to "try to understand" (as Phillips's translation has it) their wives, honoring them as physically weaker, yet "equally heirs with you of the grace of life."

Servants, masters, wives, and husbands have their special graces and special instructions. It all makes up the pattern—God's pattern. Each is as much a part of that pattern as the other, but when we think of the whole in terms of a painting, a dance, or a symphony the notion of equality seems out of place altogether. Yet husband and wife are in an intricate and intimate way "equally heirs," and their joint inheritance is grace.

# THIRTY-SIX

# *Proportional Equality*

Marriage is not a fifty-fifty proposition. As soon as it is thought of as such it becomes a power struggle, with picayune scorekeeping to make sure one doesn't outdo the other. "If I do this, then you have to do that." I have read of marriage contracts in which every household chore was actually designated to one or the other—the wife, for example, makes breakfast, sees that the children are dressed, fed, and given books, lunch money, bus passes, gym clothes and so on, on Tuesdays and Thursdays. The husband does all this on Mondays, Wednesdays, and Fridays. The wife cooks dinner on Mondays, Wednesdays, and Fridays, the husband on Tuesdays and Thursdays. Weekends are worked out according to how much outside work there is to be done, who has done the most "extras" during the week, and so forth. Can you imagine sitting down on Saturdays to add up the score? Can you image calling such an arrangement a marriage? Could it be anything but a business partnership? But some call it freedom or maturity.

What then is the percentage supposed to be?

131

Wrong question. If you were heirs together of a great-aunt's estate you might ask it, but it is grace we are talking about, the grace of life. Your equalities have been delineated: equally sinners, equally responsible, equally in need of grace, and equally the objects of that grace. That's where the fifty-fifty matter ends. You take up life as husband and wife and you start laying down your lives—not as martyrs, not as doormats or ascetics making a special bid for sainthood, but as two lovers who have needed and received grace, and who know very well that they are going to keep on needing and receiving it every day that they live together.

There is great relief in not having to be equal. Home is a place where we ought to be allowed to be unequal, where everyone knows everyone else's inequalities and knows, furthermore, that it is the inequalities that make the home work.

But inequality is really the wrong word. Perhaps Aristotle's idea of justice explains what I mean. He called justice "proportional equality." That is, justice is "the art of allotting carefully graded shares of honor, power, liberty, and the like to various ranks of a fixed social hierarchy, and when justice succeeds, she produces a harmony of differences."

I won't argue the political validity of Aristotle's definition. It must have worked in his time and other times since then, but that is another world, a world which Christians have to live with and participate in but which is not necessarily run on Christian lines. A Christian home, however, is a world in itself, a microcosm, representing—as the

Church also represents—the hierarchy of the cosmos itself. It can be run on Christian lines.

That phrase "carefully graded shares" is enough to raise hackles. Who is to grade and allot those shares? Clearly somebody has to. There must be authority to do this.

There were six of us children in the home where I grew up, covering an age span of sixteen years. The best bedroom, which was the only one that had a bathroom attached, belonged to my step-grandmother who lived with us for eight years. When she died, that bedroom became my parents'. The best chair in the living room, the one with lamp and footstool, was my father's. He sat at one end of the dining room table, Mother sat at the other. Four-year-olds had work to do just as twenty-year-olds had, but it was "carefully graded." Small ones did the waste baskets, big ones the cooking, lawn-mowing, ironing, housepainting. Girls knew which of that list were their tasks, boys knew theirs. Girls did most of the dishwashing, but the four boys took turns at drying and putting away. My mother cooked enormous quantities of good, plain food. Usually there were seconds for those who wanted seconds, but my mother somehow never "cared for" any. There were occasional complaints of injustice of the "How come he doesn't have to?" variety. My sister's idea of justice, if there was one cookie left on the plate, was "Does anybody want this worse than I do?"

If there was what my father called a "squabble" among the children, they were summoned separately to testify. The minute a plaintiff began with "Well, he . . ." he was stopped. "What did *you* do?" was the question; "I only want to hear what you did." Sometimes this resulted in the testimony's petering out altogether and charges being dropped.

This household justice was based on household authority. In marriage, if two mature people love each other, this whole matter of authority is almost entirely a tacit understanding. I could probably count on one hand, maybe one finger, the times in my own marriages when it became a conscious issue. When it did, of course, I had to remember that lines had been drawn—not by my husband, but by God. I was the one originally created to be a help, not an antagonist.

# THIRTY-SEVEN

# The Humility of Ceremony

Americans have a nostalgia for ceremony. Democracy gives us little chance for pomp and none for splendor, but you are getting a taste of those in England. Your letter yesterday told of watching the Trooping of the Colours.

"Oh, it was so regal, so majestic!" you wrote. "All those guards and bands and cavalry. The colors and costumes were magnificent. The queen mother came first in a carriage. We must have stood for three hours. A pushing, shoving mob. If it's exciting to see the queen, imagine what it will be like to see Christ the King!"

The Bible takes patriarchy and monarchy for granted. It is natural that these notions appeal strongly to the imaginations of those who have grown up with the Bible. It is also natural that some should question whether these are purely cultural and political and therefore purely temporal notions, or whether there is something in them that has to do with eternal Reality. Are pomp and ceremony utterly without meaning, merely the curious but interesting relics of a quaintly unself-critical era? The psalmist says, "Be not afraid when one becomes rich, when the glory of his house increases. For when he dies he will carry nothing away; his glory will not go down after him. Though, while he lives, he counts himself happy, and though a man gets praise when he does well for himself, he will go to the generation of his fathers, who will never more see the light. Man cannot abide in his pomp, he is like the beasts that perish."

Kipling wrote:

> The tumult and the shouting dies,
> The captains and the kings depart.
> Still stands Thine ancient sacrifice,
> An humble and a contrite heart.

In a few weeks you will be home again, and we will have a couple of weeks to talk over your wedding plans, to decide on things like the guest list, where the reception will be, and what menu you'd like, and to buy a wedding dress. In your father's biography you read his views on weddings: "the vainest, most meaningless forms . . . no vestige of reality. The witnesses dress for show. The flesh is given all the place. We Fundamentalists are a pack of mood-loving show-offs . . . It is no more than an expensive tedium." But he wrote that when he was twenty-one years old. If he had lived longer than the twenty-eight years he was given he might have come to understand the meaning of ritual, a thing utterly foreign to his upbringing.

You want a beautiful long white dress and the traditional veil. You want music and flowers and a train of attendants. Not to prove that you are a mood-loving show-off. To us, sign and sound and symbol and movement are a part of worship and celebration, and you want your wedding filled with the visible, tangible, audible signs of the invisible and transcendent meaning.

Is pomp incompatible with humility? You have heard what C. S. Lewis said in his *Preface to Paradise Lost*: "Above all, you must be rid of the hideous idea, fruit of a widespread inferiority complex, that pomp, on the proper occasions, has any connection with vanity or self-conceit. A celebrant approaching the altar, a princess led out by a king to dance a minuet, a general officer on a ceremonial parade, a major-domo preceding the boar's head at a Christmas feast—all these wear unusual clothes and move with calculated dignity. This does not mean that they are vain, but that they are obedient, they are obeying the *hoc age* which presides over every solemnity. The modern habit of doing ceremonial things unceremoniously is no proof of humility; rather it proves the offender's inability to forget himself in the rite, and his readiness to spoil for everyone else the proper pleasure of ritual."

An acceptance of universal order shapes the imagination and prepares the ground, it seems to me, for the appreciation of ceremony. We see in earthly order a reflection of the heavenly. We find in traditional ceremonies the occasion to submit to the larger truths which they represent. Your wedding will be not merely an excuse to get all our friends and relatives together to "share our joy" (as some of the unceremonious wedding invitations nowadays coyly put it) in the particular uniting of you and Walt, but a celebration of marriage, of an institution ordained of God at the creation of man, to be entered into with solemnity as well as with joy. The ceremony provides the form, the ritual which (to quote Lewis again) "renders pleasures less fugitive, . . . which hands over to the power of wise custom the task (to which the individual and his moods are so inadequate) of being festive or sober, gay or reverent, when we choose to be, and not at the bidding of chance."

# THIRTY-EIGHT

# *Authority*

There is deep down in all of us a strong resistance to, ultimately amounting to hatred of, authority. We writhe under it. "Nobody's going to tell me what to do. I'll do what I please." "Who does he think he is?"

But the world doesn't run without authority. Somebody has to tell us what to do. The question is not who he thinks he is but whom does he represent. A soldier salutes the uniform, not the man, for whether the man is his superior in other ways or not, in the army he represents a certain level of authority. He has been given rank. His rank does not prove that he is taller or nicer or stronger or more intelligent than the man who salutes him. He has in some way, however, earned his rank.

Those who call themselves Christians are people who have accepted authority. They believed God's estimate of them and received His remedy on the basis of the authority of the Bible. Jesus said, "All authority is given to me," and when He called disciples He called them to do three things: deny themselves, take up their cross, and follow. It is impossible to do these things without recognizing authority. There is a story in the Gospel of Matthew about a centurion whose servant was lying paralyzed at home, in terrible distress. Jesus offered to go and heal him, but the centurion asked Him only to say the word and he was sure his servant would be healed. "For I am a man set under authority, with soldiers under me; and I say to one, 'Go,' and he goes, and to another 'Come,' and he comes, and to my slave, 'Do this,' and he does it." It was his own experience of authority that enabled him to understand the authority—that is, the power—of Jesus' spoken word, and Jesus said He had not found such faith even in Israel. In response to the man's faith, Jesus spoke the word and the servant was healed.

In order to exercise authority it is necessary to obey authority. The centurion declared that he was a man "under authority," with soldiers under him. He respected the authority of Jesus and submitted himself to it in faith.

In order to be a disciple we must deny ourselves—this is to exercise authority over our own spirit. We must take up the cross—this is to submit to Christ's authority. And we must follow—this is continued obedience. This is the road not to confinement, to bondage, to a stunted or arrested development, but to total personal freedom. It means not death but life, not a narrowly circumscribed life but "abundant" life. The gate is narrow but not the life. The gate opens out into largeness of life. There is, we know, also a broad way. We know where it leads—to destruction.

Acceptance of the divinely ordered hierarchy means acceptance of authority—first of all, God's authority and then those lesser authorities which He has ordained. A husband and wife are both under God, but their positions are not the same. A wife is to submit herself to her husband. The husband's "rank" is given to him by God, as the angels' and animals' ranks are assigned, not chosen or earned. The mature man acknowledges that he did not earn or deserve his place by superior intelligence, virtue, strength, or amiability. The mature woman acknowledges that submission is the will of God for her, and obedience to this will is no more a sign of weakness in her than it was in the Son of Man when He said, "Lo, I come—to do Thy will, O God."

# Subordination

"I just can't stand the idea of being a doormat," Jo said when I tried to talk to her about the biblical principle of rule and submission. She's about to get a divorce because she's determined to find freedom, and her marriage, she says, was not fifty-fifty as she thinks it ought to be. She has been sold a bill of goods by those who have declared that submission of any kind is bondage. Yes, there have been great wrongs in society. Yes, I agree that men are not meant to oppress one another. Yes, it's true that some men have treated women as doormats. No, a husband is not commanded to domineer nor a wife to be servile. There have been all sorts of human bondage which the Christian ought to be the first to deplore and correct. Jesus came to loose captives.

But submission to God-given authority is not captivity. If only I could have helped Jo to see this, but when I asked her what she thought should distinguish a Christian marriage from all others she said, "Equality." Equality is, for one thing, a human impossibility in marriage. Who is in a position to apportion everything according to preference or competence? "If I like it, I do it," Jo said, "and I should be the one to do it. If I don't like it, Bill does it. If he doesn't like it either, then we divide it in half." Sounds all right at first. It's certainly the way a lot of things get done in any household, I suppose, and I wouldn't say it's wrong. But is there a truly happy household where the members are doing only what they like and are never doing gladly what they don't like? It is a naive view of human nature to assume that two equals can take turns leading and following, and can, because they are "mature," do without rank. Common sense has told women in all societies in all ages that the care of the home was up to them. Men have been providers. There are surely circumstances in our complex modern society which call for modifications. I know many seminary students' wives who have to work in order to pay their husbands' tuition and the grocery bills. Obviously the husbands must do some of the housework and child care. This is a temporary expedient and most of them, husbands and wives, look forward to the day when things will be normal again.

If we have become so mature and open-minded and adaptable and liberated that the commands of Scripture directed to wives—"adapt," "submit," "subject"—lose their meaning, if the word "head" no longer carries any connotation of authority, and hierarchy has come to mean tyranny, we have been drowned in the flood of liberation ideology.

I said to Jo, and I say to you what Paul said to the Roman Christians, "Don't let the world around you squeeze you into its own mold, but let God remold

143

your minds from within." God wants us to be whole and secure and strong, and one of the ways to find that wholeness and security and strength is to submit ourselves to the authorities He has put over us. (The question of political authority, which the Bible also says we are to submit to, becomes an enormously complicated and painful one for some. In modern times Dietrich Bonhoeffer, Corrie ten Boom and her family, and Richard Wurmbrand have had to struggle with this. It is not within the scope of these notes to discuss that question, but I mention it in case any would think that I tend to oversimplify and would use the same arguments to defend, for example, slavery.)

Submission for the Lord's sake does not amount to servility. It does not lead to self-destruction, the stifling of gifts, personhood, intelligence and spirit. If obedience itself requires a suicide of the personality (as one writer claims) we would have to conclude that obedience to Christ demands this. But the promises He's given us hardly point to self-destruction: "I will give you rest." "My peace I give unto you." "I am come that they might have life, and that they might have it more abundantly." "Whosoever believeth in me shall have everlasting life." "Whoso drinketh of the water that I shall give him shall never thirst." "Whoever loses his life for my sake will preserve it." "It is your Father's good pleasure to give you the kingdom."

God is not asking anybody to become a zero. What was the design of the Creator in everything that He made? He wanted it to be good, that is, perfect, precisely what He meant, free in its being the thing He intended it to be. When He commanded Adam to "subdue" and "have dominion over" the earth He was not commanding him to destroy its meaning or existence. He was, we may say, "orchestrating," giving the lead to one, subduing another, to produce a full harmony for His glory.

It must be very difficult for people who have not been reared in disciplined homes to learn the relationship between authority and love, for authority to them will have been associated with elements outside the home, such as civil law. But we have a loving God who arranged things not only for our "best interests" (we're not always eager to have what is "for our own good") but for freedom and for joy. When He made Eve it was because the Garden of Eden would have been a prison of loneliness for Adam without her. It was not good for him to be alone, and to release him from this prison and bring him freedom and joy He gave him a woman. Eve's freedom and joy was to be in being Adam's complement.

When Paul speaks of the subordination of women he bases his argument on the creative order. The woman was created from and for the man. It follows naturally that she had to be created after the man. Woman's secondary chronological position does not necessarily (Richard Hooker and others notwithstanding) prove an inferior intelligence. But those who rule out the possibility of sexual differences in intellectual gifts are not taking all the data into account. There are some intriguing statistics that point to biological reasons for such differences. Men seem better equipped to deal with high-level abstractions. One demonstration of this is the fact that while there are at present eighty-two Grand Masters in chess, not one is a woman. Of the five hundred greatest chess players in history, not one has been a woman. But thousands of women, particularly in the Soviet Union, play chess.

I read about this in a book called *The Inevitability of Patriarchy* by Steven Goldberg. Goldberg goes to infinite pains to show that he is in no way suggesting that men are generally superior to women. They are *different*, and their differences are hormonally determined. "It is necessary to point out once again that there is no reason to believe that there are sexual differences in intelligence in all of its myriad aspects. To consider an ability to theorize as a greater demonstration of intelligence than perception or insight is loading the dice no less than is considering physical strength more important than longevity as a measure of good health."

For the Christian, Goldberg's statistics are interesting. For the Christian who believes in a hierarchy of order, they are even more interesting for while we believe that the traditional patriarchal order is not merely cultural and sociological but has its foundation in theology, it is interesting to discover that it has also a valid biological foundation.

There is a spiritual principle involved here. It is the will of God. From Genesis to Revelation we are shown in countless stories of God's dealings with people that it is His will to make them free, to give them joy. Sometimes the process of freeing them is a painful one. It meant death for the Son of Man—His life for ours. He came not to condemn, not to imprison, not to enslave. He came to give life.

And it is the will of God that woman be subordinate to man in marriage. Marriage is used in the Old Testament to express the relation between God and His covenant people and in the New Testament between Christ and the Church. No effort to keep up with the times, to conform to modern social movements or personality cults authorizes us to invert this order. Tremendous heavenly truths are set forth in a wife's subjection to her husband, and the use of this metaphor in the Bible cannot be accidental.

# FORTY

# The Restraint of Power

One of God's purposes in arranging things as He has is the restraint of power. Both men and women are given special kinds of power, and each kind needs to be specially restrained. Husbands, who are to initiate, command, and dominate, are specifically commanded to *love* their wives. It is no ordinary kind of love that is meant here. They are to love them in two ways—first, "as Christ loved the Church," which means self-giving. No man who sets this as the first principle will initiate, command, and dominate in a self-aggrandizing way. His acceptance of the authority God has given him is his obedience to God. His acceptance of the way that authority is to be exercised will prove his love for the woman.

Second, he is to love his wife "as his own body," which means he is to nourish and cherish her. This, too, is like Christ. The Church *is* His Body. Christ's love for the Church is a nourishing and cherishing love, a love that takes responsibility for the care of her.

Did you ever think of the rules of courtesy and chivalry as being, in their essence, founded on this

Christian principle? Your fiancé, in his consciousness of greater physical strength and his obligation to care for you, opens doors for you, walks on the outside of the sidewalk, helps you with your coat, stands when you enter a room. You, allowing him to cherish you, accept these courtesies with graciousness, seeing in them far more than the purely social gesture which, in our own day, is frequently scorned as a foolish making of distinctions which ought not to be made between people.

As man's power over woman is restrained by love, woman's power over man is restrained by the command to submit. Any woman knows that she has ways of getting her own way. It is not physical strength that is most powerful. It is not the ability to deal with high-level abstractions. She may be as intelligent as or more intelligent than her husband, she may be more gifted than he is. Whether this is the case or not, she also has "wiles," emotional power, and she has sexual power. These must be restrained. The kind of restraint God asks of her is submission.

John Calvin wrote, "God is the source of both sexes and hence both of them ought with humility to accept and maintain the condition which the Lord has assigned to them. Let the man exercise his authority with moderation . . . Let the woman be satisfied with her state of subjection. . . . otherwise both of them throw off the yoke of God who has not without good reason appointed this distinction of ranks."

Paul also reminded us that we are to submit to *one*

*another*. Surely there are times when the Christian husband, in loving his wife as Christ loved the Church, submits to her wishes. It is impossible for love not to give, and that giving often means giving over one's own preferences. The husband is not in such a case acknowledging his wife's authority. He is laying down his life.

# FORTY-ONE

# Strength by Constraint

Because you have heard me talk so much about this necessity of restraint in order to have freedom, you sent me this quotation from Stravinsky's *Poetics of Music*. It translates the truth I have been talking about into a musician's language:

"It is into this field that I shall sink my roots, fully convinced that combinations which have at their disposal twelve sounds in each octave and all possible rhythmic varieties promise me riches that all the activity of human genius will never exhaust . . .

"I have no use for a theoretic freedom. Let me have something finite, definite—matter that can lend itself to my operation only insofar as it is commensurate with my possibilities . . .

"In art, as in everything else, one can build only upon a resisting foundation: whatever constantly gives way to pressure, constantly renders movement impossible . . .

"My freedom will be so much the greater and more meaningful the more narrowly I limit my field of action and the more I surround myself with obstacles. Whatever diminishes constraint, diminishes strength. The more constraints one imposes, the more one frees one's self of the chains that shackle the spirit.

"'It is evident,' writes Baudelaire, 'that rhetorics and prosodies are not arbitrarily invented tyrannies, but a collection of rules demanded by the very organization of the spiritual being, and never have prosodies and rhetorics kept originality from fully manifesting itself. The contrary, that is to say, that they have aided the flowering of originality, would be infinitely more true.'"

The love of a man and a woman gains immeasurably in power when placed under the divine restraint we have been talking about. A river flowing through a chasm, walled in by high rock, moves with a rush of concentrated strength which dissipates the moment it reaches the flat plain.

And if rhetorics and prosodies are not arbitrarily invented tyrannies but "a collection of rules demanded by the very organization of the spiritual being," may we not without difficulty also believe that the restraints placed on Christian marriage answer to the organization of that same spiritual being? That they will never keep originality and personality from manifesting themselves? And that the fullest freedom will be obtained because of what look, to the unspiritual mind, like obstacles?

"For the commandment is a lamp, and the teaching a light, and the reproofs of discipline are the way of life."

# FORTY-TWO

# Masters of Ourselves

"Make us masters of ourselves," wrote the prison reformer Sir Alexander Paterson, "that we may be the servants of others."

We have to talk about self-discipline again. We keep coming back to that, and we'll keep coming back to it as long as we live, whatever struggles we have to endure. "Does the road wind uphill all the way?" asks Christina Rosetti's poem, and the answer is, "Yes, to the very end."

No woman who has not learned to master herself can be trusted to submit willingly to her husband. And that word willingly means that she does not merely resign herself to something she cannot avoid. It means that by an act of her own will she gives herself. With gladness she submits because she understands that voluntary submission is her very strength. Because it is the thing asked of her by her Creator, it is the thing which assures her of fulfillment. It is the task assigned her which, willingly performed, actually strengthens the husband in his weakness.

The husband strengthens the wife in her weakness by obeying the command to command. But he, too, must first have mastered himself. George Mac-Donald points out that the strong-willed one is not the willful one. A willful child wants only his own way. His will has never been exercised against himself. The strong-willed person wills against himself, chooses that which he does not naturally choose, refuses that which he would naturally choose. Many men protest that it is not their nature to dominate. Many see their wives as superior to them in intelligence, strength of character, physical endurance, or spiritual perception, and use this as an excuse to let them lead. But the roles are not assigned on the basis of capability. They were determined at the beginning of Creation to be a man's role and a woman's role and again, we are not free to experiment, tamper with, or exchange them.

It takes self-discipline and it takes humility to do your job. We can count on the God who issued the order to provide the strength to carry it out. No man has sufficient strength in himself properly to be the head of his wife. No woman can rightly submit to his headship. It takes grace, and grace is a gift, but we are to use the means of grace. Self-discipline helps. Prayer helps. Christ, who is the Head of all of us, stands ready to help any man or woman who asks Him.

# FORTY-THREE

# A Universe of Harmony

In the evenings here in my cottage on the Cape I have been reading a book about the Cape, Henry Beston's *The Outermost House*. It tells in exquisite language of a year he spent on Cape Cod's Great Beach, alone in a house on the sand dunes overlooking the Atlantic. The beauty and the strength and the terror of nature are described with deep understanding.

"Many forces mingle in the surf of a storm—the great earth rhythm of the waves, the violence of wind, the struggle of water to obey its own elemental law. Out of the storm at sea come the giants and, being giants, trip far out, spilling first on the outer bar. Shoreward then they rush, breaking all the way. Touching the beach, they tumble in a roar lost in a general noise of storm. Trampled by the wind and everlastingly moved and lifted up and flung down by the incoming seas, the water offshore becomes a furious glassiness of marbly foam; wild, rushing sheets of seethe fifty feet wide border it; the water streams with sand.

"Under all this move furious tidal currents, the

longshore undertow of outer Cape Cod. Shore currents here move in a southerly direction; old wreckage driftwood is forever being carried down here from the north. Coast Guard friends often look at the box or stick I have retrieved and say, 'Saw that two weeks ago up by the light.'"

Beston tells of the wonderful obedience of every aspect of creation—the winds, the tides, the migrations of birds, the rhythm and play of light, sound, fragrance, and color all moving in a perfect harmony as though at the direction of an unseen baton. One of the stranger phenomena described is the migration of the alewives, relatives of the herring which the Indians used to use to fertilize their corn hills.

"These alewives of Weymouth come up out of the sea, and from heaven knows just where out of the sea. They run up Weymouth Brook, are stopped by a dam, are fished out in a net, dumped into barrels of water, and carted overland in a truck to Whitman's Pond. I have watched them follow currents in the pond, once they have been spilled out into it. Then comes, perhaps, a sense of arrival and intended time; each female lays from sixty thousand to a hundred thousand glutinous eggs, these drop to the bottom, drift along the mud, and ooze and attach themselves as chance directs. The spawning females and the males then go over the dam and back to sea, the herring born in the pond follow them ten months or a year later, and then comes another spring and a great mystery. Somewhere in the depths of ocean, each Weymouth-born fish remembers Whitman's Pond, and comes to it through the directionless leagues of the sea. What stirs in each cold brain? What call quivers as the new sun strikes down into the river of ocean? How do the creatures find their way? Birds have landscape and rivers and headlands of the coast, the fish have—what? But presently the fish are 'in' at Weymouth, breasting the brook's spring overflow to the ancestral pond.

"That immense, overwhelming, relentless, burning ardency of Nature for the stir of life! And all these her creatures, what travail, what hunger and cold, what bruising and slow-killing struggle will they not endure to accomplish earth's purpose? and what conscious resolution of men can equal their impersonal, their congregate will to yield self-life to the will of life universal?"

Wind and wave, tide and storm, the migrations of birds and alewives are elements in the throb and swell and rhythm which underlie the wonderful harmony of the universe. We have been talking about the first thing that makes marriage work—the acceptance of divine hierarchy—which is, it seems to me, another aspect of this harmony. The man and woman who recognize that they are heirs together of the *grace of life* move in time to the rhythm, accepting their boundaries as do the waves, yielding their self-life to the Will of Life Universal (which Henry Beston didn't capitalize), moving always toward the final fulfillment and joy—the perfect Music—which is the Will of God.

# FORTY-FOUR

# Be a Real Woman

The second thing that makes marriage work, the most explosively dangerous element in our human nature, the source of the greatest earthly pleasure—even, if you ask me, of the greatest *fun*—the thing you've been wondering when I'd get around to discussing, is sex.

What a real woman wants is a real man. What a real man wants is a real woman. It is masculinity that appeals to a woman. It is femininity that appeals to a man. The more womanly you are, the more manly your husband will want to be. The Russian philosopher Berdyaev said, "The idea of woman's emancipation is based upon a profound enmity between the sexes, upon envy and imitation. Woman becomes a mere caricature, a pseudo-being."

For the Christian who understands God's purpose, there cannot possibly be any enmity, envy, or desire for imitation. Both men and women accept fully their being as the being God created when He made man in His image, male and female. Some lamentably confused people have objected to the use of the word "man" to include male and female, but the most superficial study of the language would relieve them of the suspicion that this is a "sexist" bias. Man is both man and woman, his humanity expressed under two separate modalities, and each must recognize and accept the fullness of his humanity under his assigned modality. We are not required somehow to "overcome" our sexuality. We affirm it. We rejoice in it. We seek to be faithful to it as we seek to use it as a gift of God. Unfaithfulness to one's sex is unfaithfulness to everybody, for a woman must be a woman both in her relationship to men and to other women. A man must be wholly a man in his relationship to women and to other men. The husband who is not faithful to his masculinity defrauds his wife, and the reverse is equally true. This faithfulness that I speak of is our answer to the call of God. One, called to be a man, and another, called to be a woman, become one flesh in which, as one flesh, they become one with God.

In every society there have been expectations which have been understood to apply to each sex. Of course these expectations may vary from time to time and from place to place, but the distinctiveness of maleness and femaleness has throughout history been a constant. It is only in our society that there is an attempt to erase this distinctiveness, to encourage women to do what men do. Man's work, no matter how boring, unpleasant, or difficult, is generally regarded as of more value than women's. "Equal opportunity" nearly always implies that women want to do what men do, not that men want to do what women do, which indicates that prestige is attached to men's work but not to women's. Women's work, particularly the task assigned by Creation exclusively to women, that of bearing and nurturing children, is regarded not only as of lesser value but even degrading and "animal-like." This is a hideous distortion of the truth, and an attempt to judge women by the criteria of men, to force them into an alien mold, to rob them of the very gifts that make them what they were meant to be. To subject femininity to the criteria of masculinity is as foolish as it would be to judge meat by the standards of potatoes. Meat would fail every test. For women to assume an ersatz masculinity means that they will always lose.

You are, Valerie, by the grace of God, a woman. This means you have responsibilities. You are fully a woman, and this means you have privileges. You are only a woman, which means you have limitations. Walt is a man, he is fully a man, and he is only a man. Thank God for this, and live it to the hilt!

# FORTY-FIVE

# *The Courage of the Creator*

In Isak Dinesen's story "The Deluge at Norderney" she has four people marooned in a barn loft during a flood. There are a cardinal, an old maiden lady, and a young man and woman, all of them strangers to one another. The flood water is rising, and they know that this is their last night. The young couple are married by the cardinal, and the cardinal and old lady settle themselves to talk.

"We will consider the lesson which these lovers above and before all other things teach us about the tremendous courage of the Creator of this world," says the cardinal. "Every human being has, I believe, at times given room to the idea of creating a world himself. The Pope, in a flattering way, encouraged these thoughts in me when I was a young man. I reflected then that I might, had I been given omnipotence and a free hand, have made a fine world. I might have bethought me of the trees and rivers, of the different keys in music, of friendship and innocence; but upon my word and honor, I should not have dared to arrange these matters of love and marriage as they are, and my world should have lost sadly thereby. What an overwhelming lesson to all artists! Be not afraid of absurdity; do not shrink from the fantastic. Within the dilemma, choose the most unheard of, the most dangerous solution. Be brave, be brave! Ah, Madam, we have got much to learn."

And the cardinal fell into deep thought.

Who of us, given the chance to arrange the world to our liking, would have had the powers of imagination that the cardinal allowed himself, let alone those that God had? Who of us would ever have had the courage of the Creator when He conceived the idea of sex? We cannot suppose that He overlooked the potentialities, the pitfalls, the high risks that would accompany it. He saw them all. And He made a woman, suitable, fit in every way, for man.

"Every good endowment that we possess and every complete gift that we have received must come from above, from the Father of all lights, with whom there is never the slightest variation or shadow of inconsistency."

I think it would be correct to include sexuality as one of the good endowments that we possess. It is one of the terms of our life, one of the givens, that we had no choice about and that we are not at liberty to alter. There is an underlying principle of sexuality. The relationship between man and wife, as we have already seen, symbolizes the relationship between Christ and the Church. In the family of God, however, some have seen sexuality as a distinction to be carefully obliterated. Paul's declaration in Galatians has been cited as proof that there is no difference between the respective positions of men and women. "For in Christ Jesus you are all sons of God, through faith. For as many of you as were baptized into Christ have put on Christ. There is neither Jew nor Greek, there is neither slave nor free, there is neither male nor female, for you are all one in Christ Jesus."

But the man who wrote those words is the same man who took care to distinguish between the roles of women and men, exhorting women to modesty in dress, silence in church, the use of head coverings, and submission to their husbands. He also was generous in his praise of the women who had assisted him in his apostolic ministry. He recognized spiritual gifts as having been distributed to men and women alike and set down rules for their proper use. But he strongly maintained the sexual distinction. This is what is important. Paul not only never denied sexual differences, he emphasized them. This passage in Galatians refers to what happens to a Christian through baptism. He becomes, whether male or female, slave or free, Jew or Greek, a son. He enjoys the same privileges which all sons of God enjoy. But this "order of redemption" does not unite the two poles nor displace the "order of creation," as is shown by Paul's reference to this order in 1 Timothy, "Let a woman learn in silence with all submissiveness. I permit no woman to teach or to have authority over man; she is to keep silent. For Adam was formed first, then Eve."

It is a misguided kind of super-spirituality that attempts to erase all distinctions between Christians. It is a form of escapism, an evasion of responsibility, and a serious distortion of truth.

Thank the Giver of this great gift, Valerie! Don't join those who apologize for it or want to make you forget it. It wasn't your idea to begin with—it was your Creator's, and what a courageous Creator He is! Your obedience to Him will help other women to be women, men to be men.

# FORTY-SIX

# The Inner Sanctum

God did not limit the gift of sexuality to those who He foreknew would marry. But the gift of sexual intercourse He ordained exclusively for those who marry. This is unequivocal in Scripture. There are no exceptions. Intercourse without total commitment for life is demonic. This supreme intimacy was mysterious even to Paul, who wrote, "Husbands should love their wives as their own bodies . . . The two shall become one. This is a great mystery, and I take it to mean Christ and the Church." (No one who "hated women" could possibly have written that.)

No stronger language could have been found to denote the intimacy which exists between Christ and His Bride. Unquestionably it is because of these mysteries that physical union is reserved for husband and wife, two who have given themselves unconditionally to one another before God and the world. They enter into "knowledge" which no one else is permitted to enter. It is the inner sanctum of human knowledge. "And Abraham knew his wife."

I'm not going to tell you where, how, or when to do

it. I'm not going to tell you what to wear. I'm leery, as you know, of getting too technical. There was a man in one of my Greek classes when I was in college who, when we would be discussing at great length some particle or mood in a New Testament passage, would mutter, "If you get too technical you're going to miss the blessing." As with New Testament Greek, so with sex. Beware of the how-to-do-it books. There is danger in analysis. You can't learn the meaning of a rose by pulling it to pieces. You can't examine a burning coal by carrying it away from the fire. It dies in the process. There is something deadly about the relentless scientific probe into the mechanics of sexual activity—the lights, cameras, artificial organs and instruments, the note-taking observers and the horrifyingly detailed reports published for the world's delectation—to say nothing of the volunteers who participate in the collective experiments, willingly exhibiting themselves for the cause of science and reducing this precious gift not merely to banality but to a bodily function as devoid of meaning for the human being as it is for an animal.

It's all "perfectly natural," we're reminded, and it is therefore supposed to follow that mystery, silence, and privacy are entirely out of place. We've outgrown all that. We're liberated. I very much fear that this liberation is not freedom but a new and demonic bondage. By throwing away the very things which guarded its meaning, we have thrown away the thing itself. What was once priceless is now the cheapest commodity on the market.

George Steiner wrote, "Sexual relations are, or should be, one of the citadels of privacy, the night-place where we must be allowed to gather the splintered, harried elements of our consciousness to some kind of inviolate order and repose.

"The new pornographers subvert this last vital privacy; they do our imagining for us. They take away the words that were of the night and shout them over the rooftops, making them hollow. The images of our love-making, the stammerings we resort to in intimacy, come prepackaged . . . Our dreams are marketed wholesale."

You can buy textbooks, diagrams, and full-color photographs of sexual techniques. We are expected to be a nation of bedroom virtuosos.

Yesterday Jo and I went to Provincetown. We sat at an umbrella-shaded table by the sidewalk and watched the passing parade of dejected, disheveled, semi-nude humanity shuffling and sashaying and schlepping along the sidewalk in search of a good time. The nudity is not supposed to move us. We are asked to behold without shock, without even surprise, the nearly total exposure of every conceivable shape and size of physique. But I don't *want* to look at nudity without emotion. I want it reserved to enhance, not exhibited to destroy, the depth of individual experience. I feel I am being robbed of the incalculably valuable treasures of delicacy, mystery, and sophistication. Modesty was a system of protection. But the alarms have all been disconnected. The house is wide open to plunder.

The distinction between intimacy and openness is

rubbed out altogether. The craze for "sensitivity" and "sharing" has done its pernicious work. There is no longer a sense of occasion or appropriateness. What ought to be hidden is displayed. What ought to be whispered or covered in silence is shouted. What ought to be kept back for a chosen time, a chosen place, and a chosen individual is thrown out into the thoroughfare.

Sex is not the most important thing that makes a marriage work. But it is important. It has no authority of its own. It cannot lead to freedom. It must not control. It cannot finally fulfill. In love's highest ecstasies the lover knows that this is not all there is. The closest closeness is not close enough. The "I-thou" that we thought was ultimate brings us ultimately to that other Thou. It is the will of God that leads to freedom. It is the will of God that finally fulfills. "The world and all its passionate desires will one day disappear, but the man who is following God's will is part of the permanent and cannot die."

But sex is a part of the will of God for husbands and wives. It is one way in which they glorify Him (think of it!). They are not to deny it to one another. Love your husband, love his body, love to be close. Read the beautiful Song of Songs, a love poem included in the inspired Word of God (would we have thought a love poem belonged in the Bible?) which describes the beauties of the lover in the eyes of the beloved, and of the beloved in the eyes of the lover. They *saw* each other. His head, his hair, his eyes, his cheeks, his lips, his arms, his body, his legs,

168

his appearance, his speech are all cited with rapture. "My beloved is all radiant and ruddy, distinguished among ten thousand." This woman had eyes to see, a heart to love, and the ability to put it into words.

Perhaps all three of these things need (in some women more than in others) to be learned, but I believe they can be learned. A wife needs eyes to see the man, in all his aspects, which God has given her. She needs a heart trained by practice to love him. She needs to be able to express what she sees and how she loves. We are human beings, made of flesh and blood as well as of brains and emotions. The Word had to be made *flesh* before we could truly understand what God was like. A man prefaces his proposal of marriage with a declaration of love—"In the beginning was the Word." He says it in as many ways as he can think of—words, gestures, looks, gifts, flowers. But it is not until he marries the woman that the word finally becomes flesh, and his love is expressed most fully. But then the flesh must again become word. Both the woman and the man need to be told, and told again and again and again, that they are loved. "Behold, thou art fair, my love. There is no spot in thee." Word, then flesh, then word, and so on through life.

The essence of sexual enjoyment for a woman is self-giving. Give yourself wholly, joyfully, hilariously. (Have we ever talked about the hilarity of sex? No one had prepared me for how rollicking it can be at times!) Neither husband nor wife should withhold this pleasure from the other except by mutual agreement for a limited time. His body belongs now to you, yours to him. Each has "power" over the other's, each holding the other's in holiness and honor under God. You will find that it is impossible to draw the line between giving pleasure and receiving pleasure. If you put the giving first, the receiving is inevitable.

There are times when you will find it impossible to give, and your husband, in love to you, does not demand. There are times when you will be ravenously hungry and he will want nothing so much as to go to bed and go at once to sleep. Your love, then, will want what he wants more than what you wanted yourself. This is another kind of giving.

You will want to bring forth, for your lover, your own treasures. They are not to be revealed ahead of time to him nor in retrospect to anyone else. These are your own gifts, unique and exceptional and not to be delivered over to the commonplace. Hold them sacred. As Rabindranath Tagore wrote, "My moments signed by God need not be appraised in the marketplace."

It will not always be clearcut and simple. In this matter, as in all others where your life is bound closely to your husband's, you will sometimes be aware that you need help. Remember first that love itself—the "educated heart"—has a way of teaching you what to do. Worry is worse than useless, it's destructive. Paul wrote, "Don't worry over anything whatever, tell God every detail of your needs in earnest and thankful prayer, and the peace of God which transcends human understanding will keep constant guard over your hearts and minds as they rest in Christ Jesus." It's God who thought up sex. "Every detail of your needs" includes sexual ones. You can talk to Him about them. You can't shock or embarrass Him. "If any of you does not know how to meet any particular problem he has only to ask God, who gives generously to all men without making them feel foolish or guilty."

# FORTY-SEVEN

# Loyalty

A third thing that makes a marriage work, in addition to the acceptance of hierarchical order and the proper use of sex, is loyalty. Loyalty is based on pride, the right sort of pride that recognizes intrinsic worth in the country or institution or place or person which is the object of loyalty.

We have seen women who are manifestly not loyal to their husbands. I do not mean that they are unfaithful, but that they are not proud to be their wives. Sometimes this is because they despise them. Sometimes it is old-fashioned jealousy. A friend complained to me that she was tired of being a nobody. She was only "Mick's wife." Mick was prominent in certain circles, a highly attractive man, very successful. Plenty of women would have considered it quite enough to go through life as Mick's wife, but Liza wanted to be Liza. She was pretty, she was likable, she was thought of as a good match for Mick but it wasn't enough to suit her. It seems to me that a woman ought to be willing to take this risk. When she takes her husband's name she consents to be known as his wife. Nothing thrilled me more than to be identified with a particular man. I didn't mind if people thought of me as his wife, I loved it. I never felt that my own personality was "submerged." I was proud of his, and knew that a new personality, the personality of the marriage itself, is created when two people wed.

Pride involves identity. You must identify yourself with someone in order to be proud of him. We are proud of American achievements only because we are Americans. We are proud of the local football team and say "we" won.

In the doodles I've found on your desk and on the telephone pad I see your new name, written many times and with many flourishes. You can hardly wait to acquire this new identity. You have already begun to think of yourself as his and you want the world to know it.

This loyalty will bring you suffering. You have asked for specifics when I have talked to you about the suffering that love may entail. Here's one of them. If you are proud of your man and loyal to him you will suffer when he is criticized. No man in a public position escapes criticism and you must stand by him when it comes. You will know sometimes that the criticism is a just one and because you are loyal you will suffer the more. You will be, by your identification with this man, included in the criticism.

When he fails you cannot be proud of his failure, but you can be loyal. You can maintain that faith in the idea that God had when He made him, and you can comfort and support him, giving him the strength of your love and the incentive which your pride in him will always instill.

"For when all things were made, none was made better than this: to be a lone man's companion, a sad man's cordial, a chilly man's fire . . . There is no herb like it under the canopy of heaven."

# *Love Is Action*

The summer solstice has just passed, and the days are long and sunny and clear. It is evening, and hardly a ripple moves on the harbor. The slate-blue of the darkening sky is reflected in the slate-blue water. The boats lying at anchor are struck full gold with the setting sun, and Morris Island across the harbor is velvet green-gold in the late light, standing against the twilight. A white seagull floats quietly on the surface of the dark water near the shore. The honeysuckle makes the air sweet with the gift of its perfume. A small boat comes in from the sea, "snipping through the water like a pair of scissors."

I have only a few more days in this lovely place. You are in Oxford now, beautiful old Oxford with its narrow streets, its bells, its green and flowered closes, its libraries and chapels and halls. But I picture you here with me, sitting in the cottage by the fireplace, talking. On the mantel are a black wooden decoy, a brown pottery jug of winter grasses, a copper bowl and a row of books which are my great temptation when I am trying to write. MacDuff lies just outside the back door, on the cool brick of the patio, his hind paws stretched out behind, bottoms up, like little rubbery flowers, his black shiny nose resting between his two front paws, ears alert.

We would talk about the fourth thing—love. It is not fourth in priority. I have not arranged these in order of importance because, quite simply, I don't know how. The ideal marriage, I think, cannot do without any one of them. There must be acceptance of the hierarchical order, there must be sex, there must be loyalty and pride, and there must be, in and through all, love.

You have fallen in love. You've had the experience nearly everyone dreams of, that the poets have written about, that happens to some "at first sight," to others slowly, and to you, I think, after a very short acquaintance. I remember the first time it happened to me. I realized it had happened when I looked in the mirror, for I saw a different person there. "You love him," I said to the face, and the face answered yes. You look at his face and everything in you says yes. You know, beyond any doubting, that this is the man you could gladly give yourself to. Your heart sings, the whole world sings, the look of things is transformed.

But that is not the love of which I want to speak now. The kind of love that makes a marriage work is far more than feelings. Feelings are the least dependable things in the world. To build a marriage on that would be to build a house on sand. When you promise, in the wedding ceremony, to love, you are not promising how you expect to feel. You are promising a course of action which begins on your wedding day and goes on as long as you both live.

Your feelings cannot help but be affected by riches and poverty, health and sickness, and all the other circumstances which make up a lifetime. Your feelings will come and go, rise and fall, but you make no vows about *them*. When you find yourself, like the unstable man in the Epistle of James, "driven with the wind and tossed," it is a great thing then to know that you have an anchor. You have made a promise before God *to love*. You promise to love, comfort, honor, and keep this man. You vow to take him as your wedded husband, to have and to hold from this day forward, for better or for worse, for richer, for poorer, in sickness and in health, to love and to cherish "according to God's holy ordinance," till death parts you.

Not one of us can fully face up to all the details of the possibilities at the time we make these staggering promises. We make them in faith. Faith that the God who ordained that a man and woman should cleave together for a lifetime is the God who alone can make such faithful cleaving possible. We are not given grace for imaginations. We are given the grace needed at the time when it is needed, "*this* day our daily bread." And because you have given your word you have committed yourself once and for all. "This, by the grace of God, I will do." Nothing that has ever been worth doing has been accomplished solely through feelings. It takes action. It takes putting one foot in front of the other, walking the path you have agreed together to walk.

The underlying principle of love is self-giving. It seems to me that this is inevitable for a woman who truly loves. You already know how deeply, how urgently you long to give yourself to your husband. It is the essence of femininity to give. Perhaps it is more difficult for a man to give himself, but both husband and wife must learn this. In the wife, this takes the form of submission. Paul never needed to command wives to love. Apparently he thought they would do that without his admonition. But he reminded them that their love was to take the form of submission. When in the course of daily life the love which they so naturally feel for their husbands is not sufficient for the wear and tear, the action then required is submission.

But Paul knew that a man's love was of a different sort. His virile drive for domination, God-given and necessary in fulfilling his particular masculine responsibility to rule, renders it more difficult for him to lay down his life. So Paul imposed the heaviest burden on the man when he commanded him to love his wife as Christ loved the Church.

"You wives must learn to adapt yourselves to your husbands, as you submit yourselves to the Lord, for the husband is the 'head' of the wife in the same way that Christ is the head of the Church and savior of his body. The willing subjection of the Church to Christ should be reproduced in the submission of wives to their husbands. But, remember, this means that the husband must give his wife the same sort of love that Christ gave to the Church, when he sacrificed himself for her. Christ gave himself to make her holy, having cleansed her through the baptism of his Word—to make her an altogether glorious Church in his eyes. She is to be free from spots, wrinkles or any other disfigurement—a Church holy and perfect.

"Men ought to give their wives the love they naturally have for their own bodies. The love a man gives his wife is the extending of his love for himself to enfold her.

"In practice what I have said amounts to this: let every one of you who is a husband love his wife as he loves himself, and let the wife reverence her husband."

# FORTY-NINE

# Love Means a Cross

When you are not yet married, or when your marriage is over and you look back on those years with longing, it is without doubt quite possible to idealize it. But there is one thing which enters into all of life, one thing which will keep us from idealizing life's best and will make bearable life's worst, and that is the Cross. The Cross must enter into marriage. "Who loveth suffereth too."

The Cross enters the moment you recognize a relationship as a gift. The One who gives it may withdraw it at any time, and, knowing this, you give thanks in the receiving. Desiring above all else to do the will of God, you offer back to Him this greatest of all earthly gifts as an oblation, lifted up in worship and praise, with faith that in the offering it will be transformed for the good of others.

This is what sacrifice means. This is why the Cross of Christ "towers o'er the wrecks of time." Love is sacrificial. Sacrifice is a giving, an offering up, and the meaning of sacrifice in the Bible is the giving of life to another.

I believe you may together offer up, as a couple,

your love to God for His transforming work. You may read with special meaning Paul's word to the Romans, "With eyes wide open to the mercies of God, I beg you, my brothers, as an act of intelligent worship, to give him your bodies, as a living sacrifice, consecrated to him and acceptable by him. Don't let the world around you squeeze you into its own mold, but let God remold your minds from within, so that you may prove in practice that the plan of God for you is good, meets all His demands, and moves toward the goal of true maturity."

Maturity starts with the willingness to give oneself. Childishness is characterized by self-centeredness. It is only the emotionally and spiritually mature who are able to lay down their lives for others, those who are "masters of themselves that they might be the servants of others."

The specific ways in which the great principle of the Cross works in daily living are expressed most perfectly in the Love Chapter of the Bible, 1 Corinthians 13. Here we find proof of the stark and sacrificial rather than emotional character of love.

Christian love is action. It is the warp and woof of marriage, and because marriage itself is a life-work, this love is worked out through all the days and years of marriage, growing as it is practiced, deepening as cares and responsibilities deepen, and turning, at the same time, those cares and responsibilities (and even the drudgeries) into deeper joy.

Paul said that it is not eloquence, it is not the gift of prophecy or knowledge or even knowing the very secrets of God, it is not absolute faith that matters ultimately. It is love. If I know your heart at all, I know that you are not tempted to think of yourself as possessing any of these lofty and enviable gifts. But you do love. Of that you are perfectly sure. Will it last? It will, if it is the kind of love of which Paul speaks.

*This love of which I speak is slow to lose patience—it looks for a way of being constructive.* A girl wrote to me last year asking advice about her behavior toward her fiancé. She was already wondering how to rebuke him. I gave her this verse. You can't, of course, be constructive if you don't perceive weakness. But when you recognize a place where a little construction or reinforcement is needed you can begin to build up, to encourage, to strengthen. Don't lose patience. Building takes a long time and you have to put up with many delays and inconveniences and a lot of rubble in the process.

*Love is not possessive.* If God has given you to each other "to have and to hold" how can you not be possessive? By remembering first that it is a gift, and second, by remembering the limitations of the gift. God has given you to each other in a particular way for a particular time. He is still Master of each of you, and it is first of all to Him that you answer. There is a possessiveness which is greed, a clutching, clinging lust that overwhelms and overpowers. There is no faith in this kind, no thanksgiving, no reverence for the person made in the image of God. He is treated as an owned object to be disposed of at the will of the owner. There is fear of loss—he might get away or be taken away. Trust the God who gave him to you, believe Him to keep you both.

*Love is not anxious to impress nor does it cherish inflated ideas of its own importance.* It doesn't need to do either. You have already impressed him. You are enormously important to him. There is no question about that. Accept the fact and be at rest with him. Be meek, acknowledging that there are areas in his life where he can do without you.

*Love has good manners and does not pursue selfish advantage.* Courtesy has been defined as "a lot of petty sacrifices." A husband forsaking his comfortable chair for a moment when his wife walks into the room, jumping out of the car in the rain to open the door for her, or pushing her chair in at the table shows by these gestures (which cost him a little) not that she is helpless and in need of physical assistance, but that he cares about her. She is pleased to be recognized in these special ways, and he is pleased because she is pleased. It's a small price to pay for a warm feeling. It's another little tug on the cords that bind them together.

*Love is not touchy.* Love is touched—that is, it is deeply sensitive to the feelings of another, sad when he is sad, hurt when he is hurt, glad when he is glad. But love is not touchy. Touchiness refers to the reaction to another's treatment. When two people are living in love they operate on the assumption that love is at the bottom of whatever treatment they get. This eliminates a lot of potential hurts. It's true that it's always easier to hurt someone you love because everything you do and say matters so intensely to him. But to react in an injured way is touchiness. Love is not touchy. Love gives the benefit of the doubt. And even if doubt persists, react in love. Don't pay back evil for evil.

*Love does not keep account of evil or gloat over the wickedness of other people. On the contrary, it is glad with all good men when truth prevails.* Refuse absolutely to compile a list of offenses which you can dump on your husband someday when he complains about something you've done. Love keeps a clean slate. This doesn't mean, of course, that it's possible to forget every offense. "To forgive is human, to forget divine." You may have to forgive him when he hurts you and then forgive him again and every single time you remember the offense even if it springs to mind four hundred and ninety times. You'll find that forgiveness is not nearly so much of a full-time job as resentment.

*Love knows no limit to its endurance, no end to its trust, no fading of its hope; it can outlast anything. It is, in fact, the one thing that still stands when all else has fallen.*

These are the ground rules. This is how this thing called love really works—in a marriage, in the world.

In the intimacy of marriage you offer yourself, continually and gladly. When you give yourself to your husband you are actually giving him life. You are putting meaning into his life which was not there before and willy-nilly (this is one of the most astonishing and beautiful of the inescapable facts) you find meaning in your own life because of this sacrifice. Your husband, loving you as Christ loved the Church, that is, laying down his life for you, gives you life and puts meaning into his own. An inexorable spiritual principle is set in motion. It is not the laying down that occupies your thoughts, it is the joy. Christ, when He endured the Cross, knew the joy that was set before Him.

You can't talk about the idea of equality and the idea of self-giving in the same breath. You can talk about partnership, but it is the partnership of the dance. If two people agree to dance together they agree to give and take, one to lead and one to follow. This is what a dance is. Insistence that both lead means there won't be any dance. It is the woman's delighted yielding to the man's lead that gives him freedom. It is the man's willingness to take the lead that gives her freedom. Acceptance of their respective positions frees them both and whirls them into joy.

If you can understand your womanhood, Valerie, in this light, you will know fullness of life. Hear the call of God to be a woman. Obey that call. Turn your energies to service. Whether your service is to be to a husband and through him and the family and home God gives you to serve the world, or whether you should remain, in the providence of God, single in order to serve the world without the solace of husband, home, and family, you will know fullness of life, fullness of liberty, and (I know whereof I speak) fullness of joy.

# Scripture References

165       Ephesians 5:28, 31, 32 RSV

168       1 John 2: 17 JBP

169       Song of Solomon 5:10 RSV

170–171 Philippians 4:6, 7 JBP

171       James 1:5 JBP

178–179 Ephesians 5:22–28, 33 JBP

181       Romans 12:1, 2 JBP

182ff.   Verses in italics all from
           1 Corinthians 13 JBP
           RSV = Revised Standard Version
           AV = Authorised Version
           JBP = J. B. Phillips (*The New Testament in Modern English*)

# Notes

Page

26      Isak Dinesen, *Out of Africa* (New York: Random House, 1972), Modern Library Edition, p. 261.

36, 37  Luther's letter to Wolfgang Reissenbusch, March 27, 1525. *Library of Christian Classics*, Vol. XVIII (Philadelphia: Westminster Press).

43      Episcopal Hymnal. Whittier; hymn 435.

52, 53  Margaret Mead, *Anthropologist at Work* (New York: Houghton-Mifflin, 1959), p. 120. Quoted in Ms. Mead's review of her book *Ruth Benedict* in *New Yorker* magazine February 3, 1975.

59, 60  Essay by Kathy Kristy, used by permission.

76      Karl Barth, *Church Dogmatics* (Edinburgh: Clark (T&T) Ltd, 1975)
        Vol. III, The Doctrine of Creation.

79      General Confession, *Book of Common Prayer* (Oxford University Press).

81      Sara Teasdale, "Appraisal."

120     Hooker, *Ecclesiastical Polity*, Book V, Section XXIII (London, Sidgwick & Jackson).

137     C. S. Lewis, *A Preface to Paradise Lost* (Oxford: Oxford University Press, 1960).

146     Steven Goldberg, *The Inevitability of Patriarchy* (New York: William Morrow & Company, Inc., 1973), p. 198.

149     John Calvin, *Commentary on First Epistle to the Corinthians* (Edinburgh: St. Andrew Press, 1960).

151, 152 Igor Stravinsky, *The Poetics of Music* (London: Harvard University Press, 1970).

155–157 Henry Beston, *The Outermost House* (New York: Rinehart and Company, 1928), pp. 56, 57, 161–163, 166, 167.

161, 162 Isak Dinesen, "The Deluge at Norderney", from *Seven Gothic Tales*, Modern Library Edition (London: Putnam & Co., 1969).

167 George Steiner, *Language and Silence* (New York: Atheneum Press, 1967), pp. 76, 77.

174 Charles Kingsley, *Westward Ho* (Glasgow: Blackie & Son Ltd., 1958).